# Love Thoughts

## Learning to love, While trying to live

SYLVESTER HUBBARD III

First published by Dog Ear Publishing
4010 W. 86th Street, Ste H
Indianapolis, IN 46268
www.dogearpublishing.net

ISBN: 978-1-4575-1057-1

This book is printed on acid-free paper.

Printed in the United States of America

*To the heart and soul of women everywhere that have sought the love of a man and failed to receive his love in return. And to every man that reads this book, may he find it within his heart to love every woman to the fullest of his ability.*

# TABLE OF CONTENTS

**Chapter IV** - Love does not always manifest itself in smiles & laughter.

**Chapter V** - Giving up is not an option, if moving on is still possible.

**Chapter VI** - Love is capable of healing the bruises of failure.

# ACKNOWLEDGEMENTS

*To my friend, Karita Bell, for her willingness to be a sounding board and for her listening to my thoughts with an open mind.*

*To my wonderful sister, Tina Williams, for unknowingly loving me through my lonely moments.*

# INTRODUCTION

*I AM ON A JOURNEY. It did not start with the writing of this book, nor will it end with this book's completion. It continues to be a challenge for me to learn who I am and how I am to interact with others. I have walked alone yet I have followed in the footsteps of many others. This walk I am alluding to has been slow at times, but it is not due to my level of patience. I have just been slow to learn and even slower to adjust. Meditation and deep thought has done little to speed up this learning process. This process of trying to live life to the fullest, to love unconditionally and to give my very best for the sake of a relationship.*

*I have written many things in the hopes of opening up my own eyes to the ins and outs of interpersonal relationships. I am far from an authority on the subject, but I am not afraid to put my thoughts out there to be scrutinized. I welcome it. What you should realize is that each poem in this book took less than twenty minutes to write. I say that not to boast or for it to be viewed as a badge of honor. I mention it simply for you to be aware that what you will read will be an incomplete assessment of a thought. A critique, if you will, of an emotion that has occurred in my mind at a given point in time, based on a specific event. Like a court reporter, I am simply scribing events based on this slow-motion video of life. Writing as fast as I can to document things that I am seeing, feeling, or perceiving. Things that have potentially changed our lives or possibly be a catalyst for a change that we may one day make. These writings serve to ignite our passions and press upon our greater selves to become a more loving person. To shape our desires to be understanding and considerate in our relationships. But, most importantly, to help us to recover from our broken hearts so that we may once again love unconditionally.*

*I also feel it necessary to inform you that I am not the man behind the words that you will read. I wrote the words but I am not yet a true representation of the words that I have written. I am still trying to live up to being the man that I am destined to be. I have fallen short on every occasion and I continue on with my efforts to break this cycle of failure, on my every new occasion. Although my*

*failures have made me wiser, my wisdom will always be incom-
plete and flawed in some fashion. Not just because each of us are a
work in progress, but also because our thoughts themselves are
biased and self-serving. As it is in this book, many will question my
opinions as well as my reasoning. Again, this is not just expected,
it is welcomed. The pendulum swings in both directions, yet my
words will appear to be slanted on the side of men. This is, without
question, true. On occasion, I have tried to stand in the shoes of
women and I have fallen short. I ask only that you accept that I am
a man and as such, I am limited in my understanding of women.
Look past this defect and open your mind to the thoughts that I am
trying to express. Because, should you ever want to understand us,
it is in my opinion that you recognize that change starts from
within.*

*Finally, I respectfully ask that you read this book with an open
mind and an understanding heart. Being sure to question or chal-
lenge those things that will stretch your imagination. As it is in life,
we don't experience emotions in a vacuum and we don't always see
ourselves as we believe others see us. So, be selective in the order in
which you read these writings and stand in my shoes for just a
moment. I encourage you through your reading, to relive those
events that have helped shape each of us in our quest to become a
better person.*

     ◖◗ *Sylvester Hubbard III*

# CHAPTER I

*Depression begins with feelings of loneliness*

### The writer
*I am not my words, but my words are who I want to be.*

### Statue
*We each envision ourselves to be less then what we believe we are meant to be.*

### Moments
*Decisions made in the moment, never survives the strains of time.*

### Alone again
*Your best friend is not always found in another person.*

### Hopeless
*It is the feeling of hopelessness that causes us to change the most.*

### No one to blame
*Your happiness is up to you.*

### Empty
*Closeness cannot be measured solely on the number of people that are around you.*

### All alone
*Who helps the one that helps others?*

### Sleep
*Sometimes it's the quite moments that cause the most turmoil.*

### Lean on me
*Your strength is measured when others lean.*

# THE WRITER

~

*Dreamers, dream, thinkers, think and writers, write. I am not who I believe I am. A man full of thoughts about life, love and living. A man trying to run from his own identity. A chaser of his own shadow. A man that is unable to change the man that he has become. A man that finds himself at the height of his season.*

*Years ago, I dreamed of a prosperous life. I imagined all of the things that dreamers had dreamt. I had all of the typical dreams and all of my typical dreams failed. I had dreams I'd live forever, never fail in any of my endeavors and make love as if there was no one better. I never considered the road life would have me travel. I never planned for the mistakes I would make, so my dreams were never practical. This dreaming did not cause my failure, my living failed me. This failure in me to make my dreams a reality. My giving up when things were difficult. My letting go when others begged me to hold on. I failed to live up to what my dreams had proclaimed me to be. I have proven time and again that I am no dreamer.*

*It is clear that my today allows me to think. To consider all of my past mistakes, to think upon my most critical decisions and to evaluate all that I believe. My thoughts are reflected in how I deal with others and are seen through the raising of my children. My thinking is me and never have I been able to escape the things I have thought. I have ignored them. I have pushed them aside and instead relied on luck, happenstance and coincidence. An unpromising hope with no works to show of. My thinking caused me to sit still. My thinking caused me to only watch as life strolled on by. Thinking about what I should do, how I should do it and where I should be right now had I tried. I was alone and had only my thinking to support me. My actions failed to live up to my selfish thinking and the outcome only served to benefit me. My actions proved to be much wiser then my thinking, because my actions refused to live based on my thoughts. It remains clear to me even today that I am no thinker.*

*They say writers, write, so that must be what I am. A man made of ink and lines scribbled across a notepad. My breathing is felt when others read the words that I have written. My dreams are realized when strangers are moved through their reading and my thinking is appreciated only when debates over my opinions have occurred. I am not real. I live only in print and my beauty can only be seen when others hear these words spoken, or when they read these words without moving their lips. I am only a fantasy. A personal hope that I will never be able to realize for myself. I am a writer. A figment of my own imagination. Hoping to become what my words proclaim me to be. A man that exists on paper, having thoughts that live in ink, with dreams that only exist on a notepad. I caution you not to search for me in these words, for I am simply a writer. You are the participant that is being written about. It is your feelings that I think upon. It is your dreams that I measure in my words. I am only the person that wrote these words and therefore cannot be found in these words. You search for a dreamer and you hope for a thinker. I am neither. All of my dreams have failed and most of my thinking is questioned. All that is here that is me, are my words, because I am just the writer.*

# STATUE

~

*I'm writing again. Not to express what is inside of me, but instead, wanting to speak out on those things that are around me. The cloudy things in life that tend to influence my decisions, my moves and my stance. Yes, my stance. How I stand, where I stand and what I stand for. I am bent, twisted, like that of a clay sculpture found in a third grade classroom. My form is flawed, my purpose is unclear and the lack of enough clay has caused me to be under-developed emotionally.*

*The child's hands that shaped me did not consider what I expected me to be. Straight and smooth, functional and appealing to the eye. I had hopes of being admired in an art exhibit. I had hopes of being copied and duplicated by children and adults alike. My hopes are futile, because the child had something else in mind when he created me. He wanted to get his work done, so he grabbed just enough clay to build something that would appear to be large. He liked big things, so bigness was his most crucial ingredient. I was fashioned taller than the rest, but it only served to bring unwanted attention to my awkwardness. He liked strength, so his idea of power came from the constants rules that his father barked at him over and over again. With that in mind, he shaped not only my body; he shaped my state of mind. My arms were too big for the body I was given and my ego was larger than those things I would ever be able to deliver. He shaped and sculpted me in the open, so he failed to hide my visible flaws. The battle to compensate for these flaws was equally matched by my struggle to hide the emotional scars. So it was bad, but it was not all bad.*

*I was able to function at my best when things were at their worst. I was strong and resourceful, capable and competent. What amazing qualities I was given that would allow me to weather and overcome the storms of life. Every storm, all storms. I had the ability to function with clarity when things were in chaos. He had succeeded in what he believed power to be, but failed to give me the things I would need when the storms of life would be at peace. Those quiet loving moments of life, this I was not suited for. I was a deformity, something that needed to be prodded and poked into* its place. *An exception of some sort, not being able to mix well with others, with relationships or with life. As the other children built cups and vase, this child proceeded to put the finishing touches on his masterpiece, by attempting to smooth out the rough edges. Hoping to make what was weird, look normal. The child mistakenly believed that his vision could be seen through the eyes of another. It wasn't and I was therefore left partial, not fully what I was intended to be and not what others expected me to be. I was strong and yet still unbalanced. Able to protect, but not able to preserve that which I had protected. Incomplete in many ways, due to the hands of this child, which was not able to fashion that which he envisioned his work to be. As is the statue, I am left to view the world through eyes of what I was intended to be, while the world sees me as I am now constructed to be. A statue of a flawed man, able to function in this life, but not able to enjoy this life.*

# MOMENTS

~

*It is in these moments, I question being loved. When my phone is silent and no one out there cares if I call. When there is no one around to fill this boredom. Having no woman, no close friend and no family members that would be open to a 3am phone call. I find myself sitting alone wishing I were someone else. Wishing I had the life of another person. Someone that has a family that has reunions, family functions and fish fry's. Someone not concerned about the job, when they're not on the job. A lover of living and not a purser of money. Someone content with life. Willing to laugh when their job lays them off, willing to drive a few hours to visit family or friends and someone willing to call their woman "baby" or "sweetheart" when her name is nothing of the sort.*

*It is in these moments, I wish I never left home to attend college. To have somehow found a low paying job that would have kept me close to family and friends. To have a different past then the one I have today. Maybe then, those that are gone would still be around, those that are depressed would be happy and those that are lonely, would now have joy. Joy not simply in being around family, but joy that comes from being a part of a family's life. Having others come home to visit, rather then you being the one searching for the right time to visit home. Having brothers to laugh and spend time with. Having a sister that will call you over to fix her car or even to rearrange her furniture. Having the confidence to show up for Thanksgiving dinner without needing an invitation, or walking into someone's' home without knocking. Family type joy. The joy that was left behind when everyone convinced me to go off to college, get away from where I was and make some money to take care of myself. The joy that they failed to tell me I would be putting at risk, when I stood at the many crossroads in life.*

*It is in these moments life sheds light on my mistakes. Reminding me of all those that I have lost, let go or turned away from. I relive these moments in my mind when I face the V in the road. When I find myself reevaluating the changes that I failed to make, which has led me down the road I now travel. If I had just decided not to change schools my senior year. If I was more open to accepting compromise and not insisting on my way only. If I had just loved*

*her for one more day and not jumped-ship at the first sign of trou-*
*ble. Had I only considered the effects on those that loved me and*
*not allowed my ego to dominate my decisions? Maybe then, this*
*moment would have passed me by. This moment that reminds me*
*that I am living with the decisions that I made. Maybe then, this*
*moment I am facing right now, would be a moment to be proud of*
*and not a moment that reminds me of the mistakes that I have*
*made in life.*

# ALONE AGAIN

~

I am alone again. Another night in this room fighting to get through another day. Fighting to keep my thoughts from consuming me. Another night with this pen, my only friend. He waits by my bedside until all of the noises in my life are silenced. He is slow to speak. He helps me with my sanity. He searches my mind for distractions, for thoughts, for things that will focus my emptiness away from my current emptiness. He is my very best friend. He is my Nyquil when my thoughts won't allow me to sleep. He is my counselor on lonely nights and he alone, is the one that I turn to when there is no one there to comfort me. When my heart wants to love and loving is difficult, he is there. I have found that I owe my sanity to him. My peace is owed to him and my ability to keep it together is owed to him.

I am alone again. Fighting the same fight with the same opponent, for the same reasons. I have no one to talk to. Sleeping my life away day after day and moving further and further away from reality. I am thankful that my friend is here with me. He does not fall asleep on me. He will stay up with me until I pour all of these sour thoughts from my head. He is a friend indeed. I am reminded of our first meeting. It was shortly after my mother passed away and I had no one to call late at night when my thoughts would get the best of me. When all of my friends had gone, when my kids were fast asleep and all that was left was this stranger writing these words. I found him there. This notepad is his couch and these words are his voice. He saw the fight with my internal enemy and advised me, that I am him and he is me.

This pen, my friend, helps us to talk to one another. He is our magistrate and when he stops writing we stop complaining. I thank him daily for always being here. For allowing me to empty my thoughts so that I am able to fall asleep once again. But unfortunately, tonight is no ordinary night. Tonight I am faced with confronting my poor decisions from today. A decision that led me to compromise who I believe myself to be. Today I crossed the line. My line. A line that I drew in the sand over twenty years ago. I went too far and I now realize that I lost my way. Not just today, but over time my senses have eroded and I am now seeing what I *have denied seeing for years. I find myself ashamed of me. Ashamed of my inability to have controlled myself. I failed myself today and it hurts. I'm broken and I am unable to piece me back together again. I can't do it alone and my friend, my pen, does not have the words to tell me what to do or how to do it.*

*I am alone again. My words have run out and my friend is silent. All of my troubles remain and my sleep is still broken. Help me old friend, like you have done on every other occasion. You are needed more than ever, because you are the only one that knows that loneliness is my cancer, of which there has been no cure to come into my life. Continue to be the chemotherapy that you have been for some time now. I want to live, so help me to find myself once again. I can change. I will change. I am different now and I can be new once again. I ask only that you stay by my bedside should I find myself alone once again.*

# HOPELESS

~

*I've stopped hoping to meet a woman that has the kind of courage to trust a man. A kind of woman that would measure me according to my mistakes and not the mistakes made by other men. A forgiving woman that has the courage to forget. To forget her last failure, her last mistake and the last man that failed to make no mistakes. I've stopped hoping to meet a woman that's ready to roll, ready to date, ready for a simple "hello." They're not easily found. They look just like the woman who is still hurting from her last relationship. They look just like the woman that now seeks comfort in the arms of another woman. They are lost in a sea of anger, bitterness and pain with no way of standing out.*

*I've stopped hoping to meet a woman that simply wants to be loved. A woman that's searching for love and expects to find it. Not running away from the concept of love, but instead, embracing it. Willing to hold it and allow it to overtake her. A woman that hears the word love and her eyes open wide, her footsteps are frozen and her heart skips a beat. A dreamer. A woman that believes in fantasies and family. Dismissing the notion that insists that love is a man's weakness. A woman that doesn't view a man's expression of love as a sign of desperation, a tale-tell indicator of crazy, or a confirmation that he must be soft. She instead finds hope in knowing that her dreams are possible. That there are men that exist with the ability to love her at her level. That she can stop just believing that "God Can" and move forward and start asking herself "Will God?"*

*I've stopped hoping to meet a woman who's at the same place in life as I am. Knowing who they are, what they want and what their prepared to do for it. A woman that does not search for that mythical creature that exists only in her conversations, which is, a man that has no flaws. A woman that wants it all, then questions all men that fall short of her hopes. All men fall short of her hopes. I've stopped hoping to meet a woman that stares at every man she meets and checks to see if that man is her future. A woman that's not waiting to be picked, but instead, one that is willing to swing her arms wildly to get attention. A get-in-the-game type of woman that won't risk her future on what is thought to be proper or appropriate. A woman who refuses to miss what can be, because of a set of standards her parents told her to follow. A woman that will take off the makeup, push aside protocol and make her voice known. Her true voice. A voice that's soft when handling a man's emotions, calm when there is chaos in the relationship and loud when support is needed. A voice that won't be silenced when her man can't speak up for himself. A voice that can also be heard when no words are even spoken.*

*I've stopped hoping to meet a woman that has a loving heart, an understanding mindset and a giving spirit. A woman that is built upon love and affection. Needing to be first, but willing to be second. A second thought. Allowing herself to be guided by the decisions of the man that she loves. Risking her identity, but trusting that it will be handled with the respect and attention it is due. A woman that seeks the strength of a man and not just the strength of his wallet. Someone that is tossing and turning in life because she is uncomfortable functioning without a suitable counterpart. Someone that feels somewhat incomplete without her lover, friend and supporter. A woman that puts love above all else, a woman that I've stopped hoping to meet one day.*

# NO ONE TO BLAME

~

*I'm back to finding happiness again. Back to my search for a peace that I'm unable to put my hands on. Still trying to find ways to make sense of my failure in order to better understand my unhappiness. I analyze each clue and read every tea leaf, in hopes of understanding why I cannot find this thing which breaks my sleep night after night. I sometimes wish that I lacked the finances needed to make me happy, believing that my search for money would somehow be my search for happiness. I would be so lucky. I continually find myself with an abundance of finances and too many opportunities. If only I was broke.*

*I pity myself on occasion believing that every man has his day. Believing that my day is yet to come and I even wonder, if it has already passed me by. So where is my happiness? I now and then wish that I had no one close by to love, then maybe, my unhappiness would have a face. Or maybe I could blame my unhappiness on the absence of such a face. I could then use this to convince myself that my happiness is tied to the love of a woman. A specific woman. A woman that somehow fits me to a tee, a soul mate if you will. So if the absence of such a woman is what's missing, then I blame my poor timing, or maybe I should blame her, for her reluctance to make herself known to me. It's a hard sell, because there are plenty of people around me to love and even more that would love me back. If only I believed in fairy tales.*

*My thoughts search for reasons why I continue to travel down the same roads, unable to deviate into a new direction. Somehow I'm transfixed on doing the same old things, the same old ways. Perhaps my past is the cause of my unhappiness? All of the failed relationships, heart breaks and missed opportunities. Maybe it's the old stuff in me that's not allowing the new stuff to get through. Like oil and water, they just don't mix. Could these old things, those old memories and my old ways be polluting my happiness? Can I blame a forgotten past on my current failures? Probably not. Somehow blaming my unhappiness on my past seems personally foolish, since I can't accept that my past somehow has control over my future. If only I were irrational.*

*Those closest to me marvel at my situation, at my opportunities and this freedom that I have. They see me and they see the happiness that they desire. They don't really see me. They see what they don't have and mistakenly call my loneliness, freedom. They're delusional because they believe that freedom does not have to answer the question, "Where have you been?" That freedom means, "When I eat, everyone I love has eaten." That going where you want, when you want, is what happiness is all about. They see only the things that they don't have and fail to appreciate the things that they do have. If I could only see things through their eyes.*

*Could my family be the reason I cannot find happiness? We are as close as a bird is to a worm. As long as we stay away from each other, the worm doesn't get hurt. So the worm must stay buried in the dirt, close to its environment and somehow hide behind poetry. Could my happiness be dormant because I am unable to wiggle to a new location? Am I handicapped to the point that I need help in moving to and from? Is this lack of support the cause of my unhappiness? Could it be that something was not instilled in me long ago and it is only now just coming to light? Since when has my destiny controlled me? I control my own destiny and this happiness that I seek. This happiness that we all seek is within each of us. Our search to find that which is not lost. That which is just beyond our focus and a bit out of our reach. Something that we believe is somewhere else or in someone else. A hopeless search that we have no one to blame for, but ourselves.*

# EMPTY

~

*My life is empty. Not metaphorically-speaking empty. Literally empty. Like there is no one here with me with any resemblance of consistency. I often write of loneliness and gloss over what I really mean. I use buzz words and typical phrases that all of us can relate to. Like "alone", "no one to talk to", "no companionship", stuff like that. Typical stuff. I wish it were as simple as that. I wish it could be explained with a single word, but it cannot. Empty. The word seems to imply that I am alone or that there is no one around me. I am alone and there is no one around me right now, but that's not what has triggered this thought. I can resolve being alone, I can address feelings of loneliness and if that's all it was, then problem solved.*

*But, my problem is not solved. I'm not really alone. My life is empty. Alone is not having someone to talk to or not having the companionship that you seek. Alone is missing the opportunity to love, laugh and enjoy life. Being alone, although difficult, will still allow me to fall asleep at night. I wish I were alone, but I'm not. My life is empty. Now how exactly do I explain empty? How about, outside of my family there is no one within 1000 miles that can tell me the name of the city that I am from. Or that, I have no family member, nor friend, that can tell me the name of the company that I work for. There is no one that can tell me my job title or the type of work that I do. It would even take them twelve guesses to pick which month I was born in. My middle name remains a mystery and if offered a million dollars, not one of these strangers could tell me my mother's first name. Empty. If I were to pass away tomorrow who in my life would know what to do? Where do I bank? Do I have a saving account? Do I even have life insurance? Empty. There are strangers in the park that know more about me then my nine brothers and two sisters. Empty. No phone calls from family or friends on holidays or birthdays. No gifts, no greetings, no nothing. Empty. My kids don't call me and although I know my daughter loves me, she sometimes confuses me with Bank of America. I grocery shop once a month, eat slim jims like I own stock in the company and I sleep about as peacefully as a pedophile would sleep on a cell block. Empty. I have no one to fall back on. I have no one that calls me on a regular basis. No one wanting the part of me that doesn't make money. I am left to live a solitary life. Empty, my life is empty.*

*So while I write these words, it is not loneliness that disturbs me, I can live with that. I can change those feelings. It's this emptiness that frightens me. It's this emptiness that questions my being, my surviving and my living. It has a voice and when it speaks, it speaks only to my thoughts. Working on me from the inside, in those shadowy places hidden from the outside world. It speaks words that encourage me to question my very existence in this life.*

*Being alone, I can deal with that. The feeling of loneliness, I can even live with that. But empty; now that's an entirely different story.*

# ALL ALONE

~

*I figured it out today. The reasons why I can't commit. The reasons why I don't love women back. Why my relationships fail. Why I can't seem to stop writing this poetry I write. It was not my intellect that made things clear to me. I had no epiphany. I didn't get into a conversation with a scholar and I didn't read any new books. Yet I figured it out. It occurred to me today when I tried to tell someone I care about, something about someone I no longer care about. My purpose was not to say something deep or even to explain something deep. I just wanted to speak on it because it was on my mind. But more importantly, it would let her in on the emotional side of me so that she could see the ingredients I was created from. I simply wanted her to understand a little hidden information about me. Something that a situation could say far better than my words could ever reveal. But I failed, because my words fell on deaf ears.*

*Today I learned that I am emotionally alone and that the people that want in don't like what they have seen. They had hopes of seeing sunshine, flowers and laughter. But what they saw was life, pain and drama. The life that I live, the pain that I endured and the drama of my past. The very things they didn't want to know about, never wanted to talk about and refused to learn about. But it was important for me to tell her. To actually talk about it to someone I care about meant a lot to me. I hadn't done that before because I never thought to include her in the things that shaped me. I had lived a life of solitude and emptiness and today was my coming out party. Today was the day I show my weakness. Today I wanted to reveal this fear I have of leaning on someone and allowing them to help me through. But, today wasn't the day I had hoped it would be.*

*I'm still emotionally alone. Fighting my fears and trying to overcome my insecurities. My words were pushed away when I simply needed an ear to hear. A woman's ability to listen, accept and understand. A friend, who just wanted to be that shoulder I could lean on. But most importantly, I wanted that lover, which says I will love you in chaos, when things look ugly and when the lights are turned on and my dirty laundry is exposed. Today I wanted to love her by including her into the shadows of my life. I failed and the only person it hurt was me. I was devastated when she failed to open her arms wide to receive me. My feelings were hurt when my words were dismissed with indifference. Today I failed. Today I found out that no one cares about what has made me, me. No one, not my family, not my friends and not the one I believed loves me the most.*

*I could tell her that I'm hurt or that I feel empty inside, but it wouldn't matter. She would only tell me that she's felt that way for quite awhile herself. That I expect her to be and act according to my rules. That I can't expect her to be a certain way, act a certain way or respond in a way that would suit my needs. She would tell me to take my medicine like a man. So today I will. I will fight this fight alone, walk this road by myself and fill this emotional emptiness with the noise of my own words. Today I learned that when pressed, no one really cares and that the only person that I can depend on is me.*

# SLEEP

*Right now any woman would do. Right now I'd give everything in me just to ease this emptiness that forever haunts my nights. Hopelessly wishing my phone would ring, or even to hear a strange knock at my door. Something to make me feel that someone is in need of me. Not the financial me. Me. The man that tries to write his loneliness away. The man that manipulates words so that the stories of his life can be told. Stories that rock me back and forth through the same emotions that I am yet to overcome. I hesitate to even say what I am feeling right now for fear of sounding like a broken record. Skipping endlessly and repeating the same tunes over and over again. It angers me. Being alone, never truly being loved and forced to watch my life tick away. I'm too smart to tell you that I hate my life. I'm too logical to blame anyone other than me. I'm bitter. I'm angry at not having anyone here. So I write the same nonsense over and over again, trying to explain the same things. I'm an outcast from my family and from my kids. The only thing that is sought from me is my ability to provide. It makes me wish I had another family at times. Another set of relatives, or possibly another life. I'm sad, because I don't have a clue as to what I am doing wrong. If I'm honest, I'm cold. If I'm understanding, I'm soft. If I love, then I'm pushed away and when I give up, I'm somehow needed again. I can't do this much longer. I can't make it much longer.*

*I guess this is what they call poetry. I guess this is what writers do? Write when the moment hits them. But, I'm no writer. I'm only writing to maintain my sanity. Writing to keep from thinking thoughts of hopelessness. Writing to understand my tears. I wonder from deep within myself, if anyone would ever be able to relate to these words. And if so, wishing that they were the ones writing these words. Maybe then I would know where this road would end. Maybe then I would see the light at the end of the tunnel. But instead, I stand here naked, cold, alone and shivering from the rain. Fighting not to give up and desperately hoping to see a light at the end of the tunnel, even if that light is a train. Just something that will give me hope or something that can give me closure. Any kind of change will do to keep this emptiness from deteriorating my mind and cause me to self-destruct. I haven't got much left in me.*

*I can't write it away any longer and if I stop writing I am not sure what I will have to face. My fear is real and it scares me. I just want to close my eyes to my today and not open them again until I know for sure that I am a part of a new tomorrow. I just want to be able to sleep at night. I just want an umbrella that will protect me from the rain and help me to stay strong. Strong for just a minute longer. Long enough to close my eyes and allow my loneliness to float away. Just long enough for me to fall asleep once again.*

# LEAN ON ME

~

*I sometime imagine what it would be like to have someone to talk to. A voice that I can listen to when the sounds around me are unable to distract me from my sorrows. Someone that will talk to me about the day-to-day happenings in life. A sound of some sort that I can interact with. A sound that is made from a voice that is not my own. A text message would even do, but there is no one here for me to lean on, just me.*

*I sometime imagine what a loving relationship would be like. How would my conversations flow? How intertwined would my life be? Maybe I need a sparring partner. Someone to practice with, to hone my senses with. Someone that will swing at me, hit me and force me learn. To anticipate what is to come and how I am to adjust to it. Someone I could practice my moves with. Moves that will one day guide my conversations and allow me to enjoy the sounds that will be heard in my life. A distraction that would allow me to leave my world and enjoy the world being lived in by others. But there's no one here right now, so I am forced to teach myself, by myself.*

*I sometime imagine what it would be like to have someone to depend on me. Someone that would need my opinion, my support and my presence. My being there beside them. Not just physically beside them, beside them emotionally. Like a prop. An old stick that was used back in the day, to hold clothes up in the air to be dried by the sun. A prop. Something used to hold something of value high in the air. A funny shaped tree branch that was hooked on one end and straight on the other. This is what I am when my silence is deafening and only my voice can be heard. When it's early in the morning and there is no one to wake me, I become a prop. A stick lying on life's floor, waiting to be picked up from the dirt. It is cold and lonely where I lay so when things go astray, there is no one to complain to. When I yearn for companionship, all that there is, is me. It is this silence that beckons me to search for a voice to listen to, or search for a hand that is nowhere to be found. There is nothing here, so I am left to lay on the floors of life with myself, by myself.*

*I sometime imagine that I am that stick waiting to be picked up. To be used to support the valuable things in another person's life. I have done it before, I could do it again. If only I could be picked up and pressed against the rope that holds your needs. The need of a shoulder to cry on when the tears of life refuse to stop flowing. I am that stick and I am only as strong as you are weak. My strength is not seen in your successes. It's seen in your moments of failure, on your bad days. At those moments when you need a voice to lean on and in those moments, lean on me. Pick me up from my silence and allow me to support you. Hang your needs on the clothesline of life and allow me to lift them high into the sunlight. Be assured that the winds of life will not shake them free. The eyes that do watch will never see them fall. It is what I wait for; it is what I am here for. Like a prop, my shape is also awkward. I am straight at one end and bent that the other. I am able to stand firm and hold those things of value from falling. Our purpose is the same. We stand only to be dependent upon and our strength is tested when the winds of life are at their peak. It does not intimidate us, so you only risk us falling if you don't lean. So, lean on me.*

# CHAPTER II

*Stop searching and appreciate what's already there*

### Searching
*If a man is not ready, he could not find sand on a beach.*

### She's never the one
*If you don't know what you want, you will never find what you want.*

### I need
*No one can get it all, but that's no reason to stop searching for it.*

### Single again
*Enjoy where you are today, because tomorrow is not promised to you.*

### My woman, my friend
*Reasons why my woman must also be my friend.*

### The answer
*Finding what you want requires you to pass on what's convenient.*

### Just a friend
*A friend, is to love someone without being responsible for their feelings.*

### I'll wait for you
*How long you wait, is in direct proportion to how bad you want it.*

### Love is worth it
*If you risk little, you get little.*

### I miss you
*Sometimes your past cannot be let go.*

# SEARCHING

~

*I have searched throughout the years for a situation that does not exist for me. A situation that would relax my mind and encourage me to enjoy life. I am looking for those things that can fill what is still empty in my life. Those things that have swallowed up the hopes and prayers of past relationships. Those things that do pour out of me, like that from a gash, on an open wound. Some call it loneliness, I call it my kryptonite. My Achilles' hill that causes my emotions to self-destruct when pressed. Retreat and run away from those that seek to understand me. A defense mechanism that is triggered when others show me love and attention. When others want to hug my fears and hold my insecurities. It's my unnatural tendency to resist. To find fault in a good situation, a good woman or even a good feeling and I'm unable to prevent it.*

*I am an addict without an addiction. A man without a conscience or a woman with no morals. I am Pinocchio with his nose broken. Able to lie, but having no lie detector to expose those lies. I am incapable of sustaining a healthy relationship. My fear is of myself, of my past and of the knowledge within me that convinces me that I should be alone. I am not afraid of love. I fear the possibility of being loved. The possibility that love is genuine, somehow able to see past my words and listen to my hopes. It is an insecure fear that is exposed when I am shown love and affection. A fear built up over time and reinforced by the insecurities hidden within me. Those hidden scars that the world is unable to hear when I speak and unable to see when I move. My fear of commitment, my fear of being loved, but most of all, my fear of letting go of my past to allow my future to find me. My wounds have been stitched up, but the internal bleeding continues. It's my invisible cancer that eats away at my ability to trust, love and be faithful.*

*It is this disease that can be seen most clearly by strangers. Strangers that are able to search their own thoughts and reveal their wounds. Those strangers that have the courage to speak their mind in a public setting. You may have heard them speak my name on a rainy Tuesday or on a cold Sunday evening. It is my failures which are spoken about at poetry readings. I am that strange event that makes the nightly news, that boogie-man that girls are warned about by the mothers and fathers. Erykah Badu called me Tyrone, TLC called me a scrub and the last time you gave everything to your man and received nothing back, you called me, "a female dog." I apologize for my deformity, this inability to embrace emotions. This failure to change, the me, which my words reveal me to be. I am the reason love can't find me, for I am nowhere to be found. So love can only ever be an occasional vacation to me, in this journey I refer to as life.*

# SHE'S NEVER THE ONE

~

*She doesn't have that swagger that my mind needs. She doesn't have that look that makes me want to jump her bones every time I see her. She just doesn't have that "you're the one" quality that I feel I need to remain committed to her and her alone. Something is missing. Something that my mind knows about and my heart waits for. I can't spell it out. I cannot even articulate it in words, exactly what it is my mind wants to see that my life seems to have fallen short of year after year? It's like a blind man looking for a moving target; he can get close to it, but just can't seem to put his hands on it.*

*They come in all shapes and sizes. The right conversation, but the wrong physique. The right touch, but in the bad situation. It seems to be a never-ending storyline of "almost there," "just about right," and "close, but no cigar." Maybe I'm standing too close. Measuring every little ingredient hoping to make the perfect cake. Maybe a good cake is all I need and all I should be looking for. Maybe there's no such thing as the perfect mate. A soul mate that could somehow sweep you off your feet and have you head over heels in love. Is that reality or some fantasy that we hope to just come close to one day? This quest I'm on to find that woman is causing me to question my criteria. No one seems to have fit the bill. Maybe I'm just being too picky. Maybe I'm full of excuses as to why I won't let my guard down and just love. I've considered that. I've thought, if I did compromise or settle for less than what I felt I needed, then maybe I'll turn my back on her one day. That I might one day feel that she is not enough of what I need to be faithful. That she may not be the one.*

*So I'm searching for someone that can blind my eyes to another pretty face or a sexy body. Someone that has my ears, my mind, my heart and my loins. I don't just want it for me, I want it for her. To be able to say "I'm yours" and mean it. For me to be able to resist the temptations of life. I want to be able to say "no." Not just once, but again and again. And when it's not enough for my mouth to speak it, I want my actions to show it, my heart to feel it and my patience to exemplify it. I simply want they ability to say, "No. I'm involved and that I've never been happier in my life." Is that too* much to wish for? Is that something that cannot even be found? If it is too much to hope for, then help me to understand where my logic is flawed. Explain to me why I am not satisfied with a good cake and will ruin it in search of the perfect cake. It is confusing to me, like a puzzle lacking a piece. Is it complete if you never find what's missing?

I have been involved with those that are lacking one piece or another. Those that fall short, ever so slightly. I sometimes wonder if I am wise enough to even know what I want. To be so exact as to push away real love and continue to search for those things that are the basis for my long held beliefs. An image in my mind of what I think my reality needs to be. A reality that changes from day to day and from minute to minute. A strange reality that always seems to convince me, that she's never the one.

# I NEED

*Someone to talk to when I'm down, someone to make me laugh when I frown, someone that can shake my problems off with their smile. I need a friend.*

*A person to call before I go to sleep at night, someone that I can open my eyes up to in the early morning light, someone to lay in bed with late at night. I need a roommate.*

*Someone that I can read to, talk to and discuss my life to. Able to accept my past with, walk with and cling with. I need a listener.*

*Someone to cook a nice meal for, buy a new outfit for and open up doors for. I need a girlfriend.*

*Someone that will massage my back, my feet and my mind. I need a part time house cleaner and a full time mother. I need a lover.*

*Someone to have conversations with, open my heart up with, some- one to discuss my problems with. I need a counselor.*

*A conversationalist, a therapist and a spokesman. Someone to pray with me in the evening time, wakes up beside me in the morn- ing time and spends time with me in the day time. I need a soldier.*

*Someone to tell me I'm wrong when I think I'm right. Someone to make me back down when I want to fight. A fulltime confident and a part time babysitter. I need a brother.*

*Someone to catch a movie with, walk in the mall with or just sit in the park with. A hand-holder, a hugger, someone that will smother my empty days and fill up my lonely nights. I need a wife.*

*Someone to tell my secrets to, open my heart to and write my poetry to. I need a listener.*

*Someone to build my dreams with, ease all of my fears with and spend my golden years with. My grow-old partner, my bid-whiz partner, my person to learn the tango with partner. I need a friend.*

*Someone to sit at a Bobcat's game with, walk in the rain with, a partner to ride the train with. A joke-telling partner and a "not-afraid-to-wear-sweat-pants-in-public" type partner. I need a companion.*

*Someone to raise your kids with, go to games with or sit at home and cry with. A never cries alone again partner, will cry on your shoulder with partner. Never let you feel that your alone again partner. I need a fighter.*

*Someone that's a friend till the very end, listen to your ideals again and again, invest in your dreams time and time again. Someone I can call a friend. Someone that my family can talk about, my friends can rant about and my co-workers can gossip about. I need a woman.*

# SINGLE AGAIN

~

*I'm single again so she'll just have to find me another time. No more hoping I'll meet her at the mall and no more searching for her in the library. I'm good now. I will live my life without secretly hoping that I'll meet her one day. That somehow she'll slip on a banana peel or I'll fall on some ice. My search is over. I'm going to laugh now, enjoy now and be ok now. I'm single again. No more searching for romance, no more eying each and every female wondering if she is the woman for me. Those days are over. It's time for me to enjoy life again. For me to appreciate the moment and realize that right now is where I am supposed to be.*

*Life has found me and it's only fitting that I give life my full attention. I have been lost, an outcast walking mindlessly in circles not willing to accept where I am. Not willing to accept the decisions that I have made. Foolishly trying to change those things that have already happened and sitting on the sidelines of life with my fingers crossed. How much of life has already passed me by? How many times has life begged for my attention? How many years have I wasted?*

*I mistakenly believed that meeting the right person meant being in the right situation and having the right mindset. I believed that giving everything all at once, from day one, was the way to show her that I was ready. That I was prepared for just one woman. That I was willing to love without restriction and able to guarantee her that forever love that she has been searching for. Is there even such a thing? Am I a microwave dinner needing only to be cooked for less than sixty seconds before I'm ready? Is meeting someone and then loving them just that simple? I have watched from the sidelines for years, learning the ins and outs of relationships. I had devised a formula based on what I had seen, thinking that a good calculation would ensure me a good result. That love and emotions could be predicted if given the right situation and having the right approach. I stood on the sidelines of life and learned only the things I was told long ago. Words that were whispered in my ear by my mother. Words that I imagined telling my own kids years later when they were about to leave the nest. "Be yourself and live life or life will pass you by." I later in life under-*

*stood that to mean, "The only thing that cannot be recovered is time itself." I now understand that once gone time never returns, so I now live today, today.*

*I'm single again. Yet in my quest to prepare myself for a good relationship, I failed to recognize that neither calculations nor formulas have any effects on influencing, what only love and emotions are able to accomplish. That wishing for this and hoping for that will cause one to never be content with where one is. That today is more important than tomorrow and that today is they only day that really matters. I'm single again and it's ok to want to be involved again. It's ok to want someone to share my moments with. But preparing for love is an impossible thing. You're never ready for it and you're never able to predict it. Enjoy today and if your single, then enjoy being single today. Love will find you even if you're not prepared for it, even if you're not in the perfect situation and even if you won't be able to recognize it when it appears. All that's required of you is for you to enjoy being single again, because love will always find a way.*

     ◖◗ *Sylvester Hubbard III*

# MY WOMAN, MY FRIEND

~

*She tells all of her friends that I am the man of her dreams. That I am the one that she has prayed about and how God brought me here at this time, for this moment. My woman would tell you that. I am known by all of her friends. They know me simply as an old friend. A man that she can laugh with. A man that knows so much about her and yet we are not a couple. Not my woman, my friend would tell you that.*

*There were tense moments when I met her parents. They had already found out several things about me. They had high hopes for their daughter to meet a good man and then be married in the very near future. They measured me according to her past mistakes and were cautious in giving me their full blessing. My woman would tell you that. I met them on a Friday evening. They had no idea I would be coming and they welcomed me with open arms. We laughed about simple things and not once did they question my character. I was like an old cousin that they hadn't seen in years and I fit in like the fourth player in a game of spades. Not my woman, my friend would tell you that.*

*We talk about marriage on a daily basis. Measuring our conversations against the conversations that lovers would have. Recording each and every moment to determine if this is where we should be. Planning events with our future in mind. Making decisions as if our hearts were on the line. Never living for today, only waiting to experience tomorrow. My woman would tell you that. We talk about whatever, whenever and we are never concerned about whomever. Our plans are for fun, for today and for the excitement of what today can bring. We hold no hidden requirements on our actions. We worry not about our feelings being hurt or our persons being used in any way. We live for today and today is what we have planned for. Not my woman, my friend would tell you that.*

*Intimacy is based on our feelings for each other and it is to occur when our friends tell us it's appropriate. It carries more weight than the physical act itself. It means, we have bonded. Fused together forever and that there is no turning back. Her intimacy cannot be given freely because I may lose interest. So it is rationed, sprinkled here and there during the relationship just enough to get me to the altar. Just enough to keep me from getting it from someone else. My woman would tell you that. We do the do whenever we can. Screaming is optional and saying no is unacceptable. The only expectation is enjoyment and simple pleasures. We are bound only by our desires to do it yet again. Distance does not diminish it. Time does not weaken it. It is always there and it is always available to each of us. Not my woman, my friend would tell you that.*

*My woman does not allow me to be a friend and my friend is what I want my woman to be. My woman does not allow me to be me. She does not allow me to have doubts and she does not accept my hesitation. My friend accepts me for who I am and loves me in spite of my flaws. She has weathered every storm and refuses to let go. So I have asked myself, why can't my woman be my friend or why won't I allow my friend to be my woman?*

# THE ANSWER

~

*I have not heard the right response to my question. I'm not exactly sure if there is one. I may need to reformulate my question. Adjust it so that it is not thought to be a riddle that needs a clever response. Incidentally, my question has sometimes received answers that almost fit. Answers that seem to address some basic parts of my question. But why can't I get it all? Why can't I get an answer the completely addresses my question. I'm not implying that I deserve such an answer, I'm only curious to know if it's reasonable for me to expect such an answer. My question is "Why can't I meet a woman that I can give my all to?" It's that simple. However no verbal answers will suffice. The answer has to walk into my life and jump-start my heart. Am I ready for that? I can only imagine that I am. I sometimes hide my thoughts in poetry as to not to offend anyone in my life today. Wondering sometimes if there is a woman in my life currently that is able to answer this question. Even describing what I think is risky, because I risk not describing the person that cares about me the most and who happens to exist in my life already. It's a no-win situation because I may not see the forest for the trees.*

*I have thought about the qualities that I want. Some sort of wish list that I, myself, would not even qualify to be on. So who am I to nit-pick another person's character trying to find the pieces of them that would fit my version of a help-mate? The thought of it only serves to highlight my overblown ego and reveal me as the hypo-critical person that I can be. So, I can't do that. I thought about this answer today and began to wonder if the answer is even able to satisfy me in a physical way. If she's here in my life now or if she shows up, can I love just her? Am I able to withstand every temp-tation that will come my way? Would I be able to resist the urges that have had their way in my life, for my entire life? Can an emo-tional love sour my desire for a cold glass of lemon aide on a hot summer day? Can it quench my thirst after a thirty minute run or a two hour work out? If it can, will I allow it to do so, because I'm not sure of even that. So, is there really an answer to my question? I sincerely hope so.*

*My physical desires have cautioned me that the answer to my ques-tion is not based on the outward appearance. It is not based upon financial stability, demeanor, the ability to love or a unique flow of some sort. In fact, the answer to my question can be found in any and every woman. They all have the ability to be the answer, but they all may not be at a point in their life whereas they can be that answer. Women tend to have a laundry list of qualities that they desire in a man. As they get older this list grows shorter but becomes more concise. It is eventually filtered down to about three qualities. Love her and only her, be honest to a fault and treat her like she deserves to be treated. Three simple items that every woman wants, yet three simple items that no man understands.*

*It's woman's talk. This is why I have not gotten the answer to my question and the reason why men have fallen short on the expectations of women throughout time. There has been no universal translator, no middle man and no middle ground that men and women can stand on together. And I myself do not profess to have that ability to bridge that gap. What I have determined is this; if I was able to reveal what a woman wants, but use the lingo that a man can understand, then that would bring clarity to us men. To somehow help women to maneuver around the defensives that men tend to put up. To somehow guide the woman over that ten foot brick wall, disable the electrified fence, neutralize the guard dogs and avoid the sharpshooter hidden in the distance. To maybe persuade men of women's intentions and let them know that their woman is not the enemy. What I would tell men is this; women want three things. A man that can love them and only them. A man that will give them 100% of themselves. A man that will never give up on them when things get tough. These are not only the things that women want; these are the things that I need to address the question that I have been seeking an answer for, for some time now.*

# JUST A FRIEND

~

*I only want a friend now. Someone to laugh with. Someone to talk with. A woman that expects to see only the good in me. A woman that I can talk with, about other women. A woman that's just a friend.*

*Someone that judges other men, but not me. Someone that is able to see the exceptions of a man and not simply the things that are common among all men. A woman that's not starving for marriage, anxious for a relationship or waiting on a provider to walk into her life. A woman that's just a friend.*

*Someone that I can take to the movies, but not call it a date. Someone I can walk along the beach with and it not be thought of as romantic. A woman that believes in paying her own way, making herself laugh and loving a man without pre-conditions. A woman that's just a friend.*

*Someone that can be special just for me, loving just to me and intimate just with me. A woman that has had her share of failures, dealt with her portion of mistakes and encountered enough men in her life that she can now see through their lies. Someone that loves to live, lives to laugh and laughs at life. A woman with a desire to be happy and doesn't wait for happiness to find her. Never worrying about things that may or may not happen. Never blaming others for where they are in the life and not looking to fault men for the insecurities they now live with. A woman that's just a friend.*

*Someone that seeks a suitable compliment to the woman that she has become. Someone that has no expectations, no requirements and no rules. A woman that wants the real man that is found just beneath the surface and will not require him to be someone that he is unable to live up to. A woman that seeks only the good in a man. The "real" man that lives within the man that she sees. A man that will open up to the woman that she has become. A woman that no longer wants a man, but instead, a woman that is willing to accept being just a friend.*

# I'LL WAIT FOR YOU

~

*You'll find me in the book store pretending to act like I belong. Don't be disturbed by my staring, I'm only encouraging myself to approach you. Convincing myself to do something that's outside of my character. It's been some time now since I had marriage-material in my crosshairs. I have had a constant flow of "for-the-moment-women" helping me to pass the time. I'm done with that now, that's why I find myself staring at you.*

*You'll find me standing in your checkout line, hoping that your left hand has no ring on it. It's not that it needs to be empty; I just need to know that meeting you is possible. I need to know that there will be no road blocks, so seeing an immediate show stopper would disappoint me. My conversation with you is my way of searching for an in. A way to discover the you that can't be shown while you're at work. Your income level is of no concern to me because I am not in need of someone to pay my bills. Don't be so quick to judge me either, due to my pushiness; it is due to my excitement about meeting you. I'm smiling because seeing you during your normal moments has me thinking about how beautiful you really are. I'm somehow able to see past your work face, your uniform and your attitude, to see a woman that enjoys the simple things in life.*

*You'll find me in the back row of the sanctuary, off to the side. I am sure to sit alone so that you'll know that I'm not married. Hoping that the pastor will preach on the subject of God bringing good men back into the church. This suit I'm wearing was chosen just for you. To let you know that I've been here before and it's not my only one. I'm watching you as you walk, as you stand and as you give praise. Hoping that I can learn something about your personality without us ever meeting. I'm wondering if you're waiting on marriage or will you give of yourself in the hopes of marriage. I want you to notice me, walk near me or find a reason to interact with me. There are good men out here and I want to tell you that that includes me.*

*You'll find me driving my car around your neighborhood hoping that I can show you the gentlemen that I am. It's not my most expensive vehicle, but it complements the man that I hope you will see in me. A man wanting to show you that he can support you. That he can take you out of your financial bind and allow you to start over again. I am not trying to buy your love. I only want you to know that if I remove your financial burdens, can you love me without restraint. Can you accept that you are special and that you deserve to be happy? What I seek from you is not your body, so I hope you can accept that as well. I am here to let you know that you are greater than your situation and that I am here for you.*

*I'll wait for you when my hormones scream for your affection. I'll wait for you when I meet Ms. Convenient or sister so-and-so. I'll wait for you when I'm sitting alone and there is no one around for me to talk to. I've tried moving around from person to person. I've tried searching for you in various ways and in different locations. I am yet to find you and all of my efforts have been in vain. So if you're still looking for me to find you, or hoping that I will run into you somewhere, I wouldn't count on it. I tried those things already and now I am left with just one alternative. I'll wait for you.*

# LOVE IS WORTH IT

~

*Is following love worth the possibility of failure? Is love so valuable as to push aside logic and reason? Can love cause you to never second guess prior decisions? Is love worth it?*

*I found what I have been in search of. The thing that has caused me to sit still when I have wanted to move. The thing that forces me to be patient when all that is in me urges me to rush. I found that calm voice, that soft touch, my own personal road-dog. It was missing for so long that I didn't even recognize it when I stumbled upon it. It was there waiting to be found and I found it. It was much brighter then what I remembered from my dreams. It is that sedative that helps me to sleep and that drug that I find myself addicted to. I am no longer first in my life, I am now second. My thoughts are second, my needs are second and my desires for my own future have become second. It's all I ever wanted and having found it, it will require me to sacrifice all that I have. I am to risk everything that I know and trust everything that I once questioned. My normal, which had allowed me to predict what is to come, that will have to change. My circle, which has allowed me to become comfortable with my routines and my tendencies, this will surely have to change. And most unfortunately, this sacrifice will requirement me to go from being "super" man to "normal" man, in the eyes of my daughter. Because this discovery of love may require me to change zip codes and leave those that are here, here.*

*Do I follow happiness, given the risks that I must take? Do I grab hold of a future that forces me to let go of my today? My mind tries to search for a compromise, a middle ground that would allow me to stay within the grey. Somehow be able to do both and not give up either. A road that I have traveled in times past that had only resulted in hurting everyone involved. A road that I vowed I would never travel again.*

*I am a first-time sky diver wanting to jump, but needing to be pushed. Standing at the door of the plane trying to venture out into the thing that I have sought for years. My instructor is not sure if I should be pushed, so she looks into my eyes searching for a clue that would tell her whether or not I am ready. She needs a sign that would encour-*

*age her to push me even though she prefers that I jump of my own accord. Her indecision tells me that I am not the only one at a cross roads. She has been here before as well. On several occasions she has pushed and on several occasions she has regretted pushing. She is not sure what to do. Just like a bird that is yet to fly, it must jump from its nest. It must risk its very life or it will never be able to enjoy life. It is a sight that her heart has yearned to see. A man willing to risk everything because he wants to have love in his life. His difficult decision has always been a normal decision for her. What he wants today is what she has fought for her entire life. A man that would jump for her. A man that would risk his heart even when his head is not quite sure if he should. She watches with amazement and records each second so that she can watch it over and over again in the future. This video of a man's heart being opened and exposed to her world as he stands at the panicle of life's cross road. Family verses career, faith verses success, love verses logic. His hesitation does not disturb her because her mind is saturated with compassion. She fights her urge to reach her hand out in support. She ignores her instincts to lay her heart on the line to comfort him and she bounds her legs to stop herself from jumping from the plane first as a sign of encouragement to him. She does this because she needs him to do it of his own accord. For him to risk failing on his own and for him to determine within himself exactly what he is prepared to do for love.*

*I found what I have been in search of and I am finding it difficult to take hold of it. Not because of my heart, my head is the problem. I want love. I want to live. I want to jump. But my head, my logic and this common sense in me act like a parachute. It gives me a sense of safety, a sense that if things don't go as planned, I will survive. It is what has allowed me to love less then what I should have loved in times past. It is what has held my tongue when communication was required. It is what has caused me to lose good women after good women because my logic took precedence over my love. This is why I must remove my parachute, let go of my logic and ignore sound reasoning. True love requires me to jump without a safety net and risk emotional devastation. It requires me to risk it all and hope that she, my instructor, will jump from the plane after me and guide me to safety. So in the interest of love and my desire to give my all, I am jumping. Do not be alarmed about the screams that you will hear. They are not out of fear, amazement or adrenalin. It is me calling for you to come save me because my logic is no longer here.*

# I MISS YOU

~

*I cannot write her out of my mind, I cannot sleep her memory away and surrogate mothers have not been adequate substitutes. Her impression on me is still as lethal as ever. I dreamt about her last night. I walked into a house we once lived in and questioned my sibling for changing what she had once set up. As I saw it, they were moving on and in my mind, I thought, why should I? I woke up thinking about how much I miss her. I woke up and was reminded of what remains to be void in my life. Wanting to hug someone just like her, wanting to touch someone just like her and hoping that my sleep would not be broken, so that the aroma of her "use-to-be," would continue to sit within my nostrils. I woke up this morning with a heavy heart, reliving my misery of losing her and fighting the reality of her never being in my life again.*

*My dream troubled me this time because she wasn't in my dream this time. Normally I would see her, talk to her, then awake wishing that I had slept longer. But this time she was not there, so it was her presence that dominated every emotion in the room. I could see my brother who is always loud; speak in the softest of voices when speaking. Yet another brother who spoke from the heart and did not allow his logic to govern his words. We handled her belongings like the flag of a fallen soldier. Walking gently around the place that so much of her time was spent. Others called it a "beat-down" shack. We knew it to be the source of our support. The backbone that bonded each of us together and the force that was able to mend anything that was broken and fix everything that had failed.*

*I am reminded of her this morning. Fighting the tears from flowing and wanting to scream her name at the top of my lungs. Mommmiiieeeee! I remember my older brother always jokingly saying, "You only have one mother." He consistently reminded me of my rushing her off the phone or my giving her less than what I was able to give her. His joking is now a curse that I must live with for the rest of my life.*

*I am reminded of her this morning. My words are gentle when I speak of her, but my anger is harsh when I deal with the pain of not having her in my life. I want to fight my shadow to the point of exhaustion. She is never far from my thoughts and my thoughts of her are never diminished by the passage of time. Her ever-present presence in my life keeps me grounded and taints my happiness. Realizing that living life to the fullest is not something that can fill the void of missing her. She is like leukemia in my bones and she is malignant. I woke up this morning in tears because I am yet to encounter a cure for this sickness that plagues me. This sickness I call, Mommy.*

# CHAPTER III

*Never force a man to answer to the person he once was*

### I'm not perfect
*Judge me based on who I am and not base upon
who you believe me to be.*

### Chickens
*Force him to be the man that he is destined to be and
don't allow him to be anything less.*

### Trying to love you
*Love is clearest, when viewing it through the eyes of the one that loves.*

### The old man is gone
*Judge him according to who he is, not on the merits of who he once was.*

### I was certain
*The exception to any rule is love.*

### Just like me
*Your feelings are not alone, they are shared by many others.*

### Dutch
*Love in a relationship goes in both directions.*

### No more lies
*...to thine own self be true... W. Shakespeare*

### Never satisfied
*If you don't know what you want, you'll never get what you need.*

### Awakened
*If you understood the power of mom,
you would second guess ever living home.*

# I'M NOT PERFECT

~

*I don't have a personality that fits your every wish. I am not strong, sensitive, understanding and loving all at the same time. I can't even say I know when to love, because I don't know when you'll require me to be that way. I can't read minds. I'm not able to hug your pains away, ease all of your fears or hide your imperfections. I'm not perfect.*

*I don't have the ability to talk to you for hours over the phone each and every single night. I'm not able to pour out my every emotion at the drop of a hat. And the emotions that I do have were not bestowed upon me like that of a king anointing a knight; I have to work at it. I am not yet able to read your mind and I am even worse at reading body language. So telling me exactly what you think would be the simplest way for me to understand how to react to you. I have no history to draw upon that could empower my nonexistent superpowers. So the special powers of reason and deduction that you believe I have are nothing more than a dream that you are yet to awaken from. I do not have the gift of discernment and my view of things will always seem to be distorted. I'm not perfect.*

*I don't have a smile that can brighten up a dark room. My body is not built in such a way that women have to fight the urge to remove their underwear. A touch from me will not send a tingling sensation from the top of your head to the soles of your feet. I am not that guy that you have dreamt about, I'm just a man. I don't have the complexion of a caramel apple dipped in molasses. I have never been described as being chocolate or even light-skinned. I don't have shoulders that were carved out of twisted steel. My chest hair is not always uniform, the hair about my face does not make me look sophisticated and a barber has never told me that I have Indian in my blood. I'm not perfect.*

*I don't have the clearest skin because I wasn't able to resist the temptation to run through the woods in shorts when I was just a little boy. Manicures and pedicures have never been a part of my usual routine. I am not the best of dressers. My ability to coordinate colors or styles could be compared to that of a clown preparing for a costume party. I don't have a divine demeanor and my style is often a dollar short and a day late. My appearance does not invite unwelcomed attention and the eyes that I have are not the eyes that I was born with. I'm not perfect.*

*I don't keep the cleanest of cars and my home is far from spotless. I don't have a credit rating that would allow me to obtain the best possible interest rates. So I would be lying if I told you that I have never requested a payday loan. I don't have a job that I can afford to lose, so I am not able to stand on principal in every situation that arises in my workplace. I'm not perfect. I don't have kids that have never fractured the law or have never spoken back to me in a disrespectful manner. They don't always feel loved and appreciated when I'm around them. I don't have great interactions with my exwife and I don't maintain the greatest of relationships with all of my siblings. It would not even be a stretch if I told you that the number of people that hate the sound of my voice exceeds the number of toes on my feet and the number of fingers on my hands. I don't have a problem with my ears, but that doesn't stop me from ignoring reason and sound arguments when loved ones attempt to get through to me. I'm not perfect.*

*I don't always agree with everything that I am told and I don't always accept the love that I am shown. Be careful when you bank on how much I will love you, because my love for you today is not as clear as I believe it to be. I don't have a soft tone when my temper is exposed and my sharp tongue is not just a feather, it's a billyclub. I am not everything that you have read about in books and magazines. I am not always romantic, loving and caring and I don't have complete control over all of my hormones. I may never be the man that lives in your dreams, because I'm not a man that has no imperfections. I'm not perfect.*

# CHICKENS

~

*There she goes passing me by like a runaway train with no brakes. Her eyes are focused on her future and her today has no desire to be happy. What about me? I stand in the distance doing jumping jacks and cart wheels hoping to be noticed. I get only a glance. A look. A piece of lint stuck to the corner of her eyelid. I am brushed away and find myself floating in the wind. My words are muffled amongst all of the other voices in her life. So, she passes me by and I am unable to catch what I so desperately want to hold on to. My eyes follow her as she seeks to get those things that I could deliver to her with a simple stroke of my pen. Three seconds of my time can deliver her financial peace. It's an easy swap for me. Sacrificing less than 80 work-hours of my life for a chance to be the love of her life.*

*She is looking for eggs and has walked right past her chicken. Her hopes are bigger then her vision, so she blindly searches for dreams that have already been hatched. Her quest is genuine though, so I can't fault her for trying. Her visions of happiness no longer require a man. She has given them enough chances. They are only consistent at failing. It's the only thing that she can be sure of. Men will fail you. So she goes on with life trying to get those eggs that can make life bearable. Functional. To smile and find comfort in the day-to-day chores of life. She has not given up on men. She has decided that she won't accept another application so long as the job requirement includes consistency, support and longevity. Her plan is to have that taken care of, thereby; taking the pressure off all future applicants.*

*But it comes with a cost. A part of her soul has to be put on hold. She has to become numb to her desires and her emotions. She has to think more with her head and less with her heart. She has to allow herself to be guided by logic and purpose. She has to become more like men! Like the very creatures she has dreaded in her past. She has to risk losing a forever part of her womanhood and in doing so she has to risk not meeting me. Not allowing me the opportunity to be the chicken that I am. Able to hatch her dreams on a daily basis, without effort and without coercion. She will pass me by in search of eggs and never know that she walked right past her dream, passed by her friend, overlooked her supporter and failed to see her old man. She was expecting to see eggs so she didn't consider the chicken. The sounds it made were questionable. Its feathers were not as white as snow. It was far from the best looking thing, but I wanted to tell her that it was me. I'm the chicken that can hatch her dreams and I don't need persuasion to do it. Because I'm a chicken and that's just what chickens do.*

# TRYING TO LOVE YOU

~

*I'm trying to love you. I'm trying to let you know that you're not in this alone. I hope you are able to see the man that I'm trying to be. A friend, a lover and a lifelong companion. I am able to be that guy. It's not too far of a stretch for me. It's well within my reach so keep fighting your urges to give up.*

*I'm trying to love you. Writing poem after poem trying to get out what's been locked in. Trying to uncover the hidden man that you are dying to see. The man that no one else knows about. The man that wants to make your heart flutter with just the sound of his voice. I write to tell you that my words are me. The voice you hear is my voice. I'm in here screaming for you to stay. To stick around for a bit longer. Don't leave anytime soon. The man that you have dreamt about is real. He exists and he is in me.*

*I'm trying to love you. Weaving you into my life at a slow pace, but weaving I am. Making decisions on what I do and when I do them with you in mind. Changing my schedule with you in mind. Thinking about my future with you in mind. You are important to me. Your opinions do matter and you are not an afterthought. I'm trying to accept that adjustment in my life, which comes in the form of loving you. A walk in the park that I had never considered in my past. A trip to an amusement park to ride rides I don't have a desire to ride. These words I write at this very moment are to let you know that you are with me. You are a part of who I want to become. You may not be able to touch it with your hands, so I am working on showing you how you can see it with your eyes.*

*I'm trying to love you. That woman that takes pride in being thought of as my woman. That believes in relationships and the sanctity of marriage. The woman that only wants to love one man, one way, which is to her fullest. That all-or-nothing woman, which wants your all and will accept nothing less. The woman that gives me patience, gives me love and gives her very best for the sake of the relationship. So judge me not on my actions alone, on my words alone, or on my failures alone. Judge me instead on the reasons why I wrote these words today. Quite simply, it's to encourage you not to give up and to tell you that this is my way of letting you know, that I'm trying to love you.*

# THE OLD MAN IS GONE

~

*The old man is gone and I am the man that remains in his place. I am of the same form, the same substance, but my character is different. My understanding is different. The way I process information is different and yet the old man still lives in me. He has become a leper in my life though. A disease that can only be controlled but never cured. He whispers in my ear and tells me how to lie. He whispers in my ear and encourages me to manipulate. He is the man behind the mistakes and he lives within me. His actions alone require me to repent. To confess to the Man above and seek forgiveness from those that has crossed my path.*

*The old man is gone and I am the man that remains in his place. We look the same, but what we look at, looks different. What I could not see before, I see now with clarity. My eyes can now see beyond skin and bones. Beyond the material that is hung from a woman's body. My eyes can now see just beneath the surface and peep at the substance that a woman tries to pour into a man's mind. The material that allows her to love unconditionally and without limits. I can see now what the old man could never see, the woman within the woman. She holds the building blocks of love within her flesh and the man is her nucleus. Her growth is not dependent on her actions alone. She needs a man more than a man needs her. I see that now and I won't be lied to again by the old man in me.*

*The old man is gone and I am the man that remains in his place. The new man. A stranger to the occasional lie. A risk taker who's willing to risk everything, not just finances, emotions. Open to the possibility of being played. A one-woman man with no taste for variety. A man willing to be hurt by the one he loves the most. Willing to be the victim in a failed relationship. He has been here all along, fighting to be the man that the old man could never be. A man sour to the thought of failure and forced to survive in a world that does not recognize his true worth. A man that works hard when there's work to be done. Doing his best to do what he should do and not what comes naturally to him. That natural tendency to be selfish, bossy and controlling. His fight does not end in the street. He struggles to be the man that is dreamt about. The man that is talked about in romance novels.*

*The old man is gone and I am the man that remains in his place. But I am never alone. I live with the constant threat of the old man influencing my decisions. I live with the constant threat of being pushed from my throne and then forced to live at the footsteps of my old man. My instinct is to serve, but my desire is to lead. To stand and open myself up to rejection, humiliation and laughter. But I cannot stand alone for long. I need the substance that can only be given to me by a woman. Her essence. Her ability to bring joy to a dreary day, light to a dark situation and peace to the turmoil in my life. The old man is gone and I am the man that remains in his place, but I won't be here long, if a woman doesn't take hers.*

# I WAS CERTAIN

~

*I was certain of what I would do today. I was sure about the things I had already decided, things that I had prepared responses for. The things that I would do if this or that happened. I had a grocery list of items that I had already prepared responses to. Well thought out responses. Responses that any reasonable, rational person would do. If she cheats, I'm gone. If she's crazy, then see ya. They were simple answers to clearly simple questions. We all do it. We plan out our relationships and have a "no no" list that we keep to ourselves. I had my list written down and over the years I polished it. It was perfect. It fit my personality, my lifestyle and my positions on how relationships should flow. My list was waterproof, fireproof and most importantly, woman proof. No woman could question me about my list or convince me to make adjustments. My list was set, I was set and everyone else would just have to accept it as is.*

*Over the years, my list secretly dictated my decisions on life, on love and on intimacy. It had never crossed my mind that someone would attempt to change my list. Or, that maybe I would wise-up and make adjustments to the list myself. Time has passed and yet my list has stayed the same, a simple list, my personal list. A list written in ink so that no changes could be made. Invisible paper was used so that my list could never be found. Code words and tricky phrases were used just in case I talked in my sleep. And a cyanide pill was placed just beneath my tongue, should I ever be tortured and forced to reveal its whereabouts. My list was safe and was protected from all manner of thievery. It was bulletproof and for my entire life, up until 10:30 last night, my list was known only by me. Like an umbrella when it's raining or a cellar during a tornado, it was foolproof. It not only protected me, if gave me a sense of consistency. It never changed so I used it as a basis to say that I am grounded. However, what my list actually did was made me rigid, stiff and inflexible. But still I had no plans on changing my list and yet my list was changed.*

*Last night my list was destroyed and there was nothing I could do to prevent it. A chemical was found that was able to turn the invisible back to the visible. My unbreakable code was able to be decoded. I was unable to resist the pressure that was put on me to reveal its hidden location and my clever phrases were countered by clever phrases. My list had been found, exposed and then refuted. I had not anticipated this agent, this thing that had the ability to undo everything that I had done. It was quick, so quick that I found my shell-shocked. I was caught off guard and when I came face-to-face with this agent I realized that I was no match for it. That had I even had guard dogs, then that agent would have had a steak to distract them.*

*I was defeated by a combination of chemicals not found on the periodic chart and not based upon elements that could be measured or tested. Love was the substance. It was able to turn my "nevers" into "maybes". My "I don't think so's" into "I think so." Love was able change the time I was willing to go to bed on weeknights. It was able to move my name from the top of my priority list to the bottom. Love told me "I will" when I proclaimed that I never would. Nothing was certain anymore and all of my resistance to the demands of love was not only shut down, it was turned inside out. Love ruled the day. And as for certainty, I have none. Only love was certain. It was certain to remind me that all of my best made plans would certainly change should love walk into my life.*

# JUST LIKE ME

~

*She's been searching for a man that has a loving heart. A man that wants to give her all that she has waited for. A man that finds himself standing in the same shoes that she now stands in. That man she seeks has a stance just like me.*

*She has made many mistakes in the past. Giving all that she has and getting nothing that she wants. Wants that are simple. Easy for any man to give, but has proven to be difficult for every man to give. To value her, all of her, in such a way that she is made to feel appreciated, equal and desired. She requires that his actions be who he really is and not just what he is able to do. She wants to see him when he's flipped inside out and know with certainty that what he gives is exactly who he is. That man that is more then he appears to be on the surface. That man she seeks sounds just like me.*

*She has talked about him, she has prayed about him and she has prepared herself just for him. She has no preconceived ideas of what he may look like. She does not question where she may meet him or how they will find each other. She, instead, braces herself so that she is able to accept the man that is right for her and not the man that's convenient for her. Someone that loves first and laughs second. Someone that she cannot put on tilt, shake free, or knock off balance. She wants a man that she can say marriage to, kids to, love to and he not run away from her. Someone that can look within her and know her without her telling every little detail. A man that has x-ray vision, able to see past her conversation, over- looks her beauty and peer at her inner soul. She wants a man that will look beneath the surface and judge her according to who she believes herself to be. That man she seeks has eyes just like me.*

*She wants a man that will accept her as well as her kids. A role model in their life, but not another dad. She wants a positive per- sonality that her kids can grow up to admire. Someone that can walk into her life and be there permanently. She has no, just-in- case-it-doesn't-work-out plan. So him not being the one is not an option. She is standing at the free throw line of life waiting to take her shot. When she meets him, she wants to be able to make her* move without hesitation and without any fear. But, fear will still grip her. Not because she is afraid, but instead because she will be facing her destiny. The man that has been molded on the brazen alter and prepared by the word of God, just for her. His arrival in her life is right on time. His ability to immediately love her will be breathtaking. Her soul will see him clearly, but her heart will still have questions. She will be like Ruth when she was found by Boaz. She will happen to be at the right place. It will happen to be the right time and she will happen to catch his eye. He may have passed by her many times before, but this time there spirits will meet and her heart will skip a beat. She found him and that man that she seeks, has beliefs just like me.

She will wait no longer to receive what has been given to her. She will ask him to love her immediately, be hers immediately and begin their life immediately. She has already thought about her willingness to love him when he arrives. She has prepared herself for this moment and she has promised God that she will love him according to his word. And in doing so, the only hole in her life which the enemy has tortured her with will be closed. She will love God to her fullest and give him all the glory and all of the praise, just like me.

# DUTCH

~

*Why can't we meet halfway, give 50 percent a piece and expect back only those things that we have given? I choose not to be the one that is putting in all of the work. I choose not to be the one that is doing all of the whining and dinning. Why can't my counterpart work as hard as me to show her sincerity? I've had enough. Driving my car everywhere and anywhere. Using my gas and putting my vehicle through the ringer. Spending money every time we meet. Since when did I become a banker? Bank-rolling dinners, lunches and they occasional late night breakfast. I do those things and all that I am given back, is nothing. Check that, I'm given back words. Some concept that women live by that says a man is suppose to do these things. No more. As of today, I have paid for my last relationship. I will never again prove my commitment by paying for this or being responsible for that. I didn't sign up for those things. I thought getting to know each other was a two-way street. I thought sacrifices were going to be equal. I thought that love was to rule the day and traveling down the bumpy road of life is what we would share. I thought wrong.*

*Why can't we give what we expect to receive, meet down the middle, or do our fair share? Is that too much to ask for? To insist that each person carry their own weight, be responsible for their own needs and evaluate each other according to what each of us has given. I have had no expectations of intimacy. I seek no hug, kiss or affection of any sort. Just fairness. An agreement to give equally in all things tangible or intangible. A shared sacrifice that each of us is willing to endure, so when more is expected, more is given. It may seem like a strange ideal, but why not try it? The proposition that everything you want you give, and everything you give you expect to receive back. Allowing your partner to be true to themselves and not force them to reveal only their representative. That robot that is guided by the relationship rule book and not by the experiences that they have learned in life.*

*Dutch. A simple word that implies fairness, pulling your own weight, meeting in the middle and expecting no more than what is deserved. A commitment to working equally as hard as your partner in building a stable relationship. Balancing the scales both emotionally and physically. Dutch. It's the desire to stand on your own steam and to give your partner the knowledge that wherever we go, we go there together. Your lost is her lost and your success is her success. Because rather than buy her love and fool her senses, you'd much rather give her an equal return on her investment. An investment that is sure to yield her a return of 100-fold. A retirement plan that would pay her according to what she is prepared to invest. A plan that can be paid for through her willingness to build the relationship on the novel concept of going Dutch.*

# NO MORE LIES

~

*I have lied to you. Not directly, but in an indirect way. The way I stand, the way I talk, my demeanor. The lie is hidden in my thoughts, revealed in my thinking and exposed in my words. It's ringing in your ears right now. The vibrations that make sounds are nothing more than my lie being painted across your landscape. It's a clever lie, because it sounds just like the truth. It looks like a sleeping crack-head, not knowing what to expect or when to expect it. My lie is intentional. I twist words so that I can convince your senses that it is the world that I am writing about. My lie is easily accepted because the truth is hard to believe. So much so, that my truth sounds like a lie and my lies sound like poetry. You're safe though, because my lie cannot hurt you. Instead, my lie encourages you to reflect upon the cracks in life. The wrinkles in life that serve to mold us, the failures that tend to shape our conversations and the missteps that have caused us to face our inner demons. This is what my lie does for you, but as for me, it's like a layer of guilt that stains my every word. Leaving me unable to reveal the man that I want to be, for fear that you may see the man that I used to be.*

*I have lied to you through my words, because I have played upon your perceptions of what my words have lied about. This lie I speak about hides "who I am." At first glance, I am a tall black man of average looks with an above average physique. Somewhat well spoken with a nerdish quality. Seemingly confident, borderline arrogant. These are the truths that cannot be changed with my deceptive words. These are the truths that are overlooked by my lies, by my twisted words, by my poetry.*

*A sensitive man by nature, I am not. I have lied and cheated and have left several devastated females in my past. I have lived, loved and been hurt. It is just in my recent past that I have come to realize my crimes. The last couple of years have brought to light all those things that my poetry attempts to hide. A sensitive man with an insensitive past. A past that I am unable to make right. A forever burden for my tomorrows.*

*A loving man by nature, I am not. My intellect is my handicap. A blue sticker that hangs at the forefront of my emotions to caution everyone that the man there approaching is unable to function without assistance. My intellect thought loving was something that could be figured out. Something to control, adjust, fix or even measure. I was wrong. I know what it is to love a woman now that I have no woman to love. I am not deserving of your sympathy. I have had my second and third chances. I have failed time and time again and I am only now able to unwind my twisted words to tell you a story that I was unable to admit to. A story I am unwilling to confess the truth to, not able to come clean with and failing over and over again from stating the plain and simple truth.*

*I have lied to you because I will not tell you that I am now dying a slow death. Because my heart has no woman to love and no woman that loves wants to love me. I have lied to you because I will not tell you that I deserve to be alone. I deserve to be unhappy and my situation is one that I have created for myself. It's my bed, I made it and I'm now not man enough to lay in it. I have lied to you because I will not tell you that I seek forgiveness. I need a ninth chance to do it right. To say it the right way, to live right, to love you right, to be the right supporter, to be sensitive in the right way. I have lied to you because I will not tell you that I want to fix it. I want to travel back in time and change what has happened, but I cannot. I am only able to look forward in time and build something for a better tomorrow. I ask not for your forgiveness, your sympathy, or for you to be in agreement with me. I simply ask for a woman to step forward. A woman wanting to be loved unconditionally. A woman who is willing to give this poor excuse of a man a ninth chance to do it right. But this time, with no more lies.*

# NEVER SATISFIED

~

*I never learned to fight. I never learned to go after those things that I wish I had. I have always backed away from my desires. I have been consistent at pushing away from those things that were even right in front of me.*

*I never learned to fight. I never ran, but I never attacked either. I was only good at waiting, standing around and receiving what was given to me. I'm not a fighter, I'm a thinker. Thinking of ways to twist my emotions so that they could absorb the blows of a failed marriage, a failed relationship, or a failed friendship. I have known what I am good at for years and fighting was not one of them. The way I have bobbed & weaved or ducked & dodged, would lead one to believe that I was well trained. I am not. I have just been in the ring for so long that instincts I never knew I had, just happened to have kicked in. Having taken many blows, many ways, my wounds have required me to adjust. To twist and turn my way around the ring until I can be saved by the bell. Having no ability to fight, my weaving seemed to be the only option left to me. To somehow wear my opponent down through frustration and boredom.*

*My past battles have revealed my weaknesses. My tendency to open myself up, drop my guards and wait for the attack to begin. This was my thing. To show others what I had and what was in me. My lack of pursuit, my lack of tenacity and my lack of a desire to spare with them. I was there but gave nothing back, forcing them to swing more and hit harder. Indirectly encouraging them to fight harder while I simply bounced around the ring making things ever so difficult for them. It was a tiring dance that I had grown accustomed to. A dance that they had never learned and never understood how to perform. This has become my tactic and this is why my every opponent has chosen to leave the ring and fight a different battle.*

*I never learned to fight. I have never been clear on what it is in me that makes me want to dance around the ring, avoid contact, dis-miss communication and then hope that something good would happen to me. It is clear that I am not in tune with the person that*

*I have become. A person that's not satisfied with anyone, for any reason, for any length of time. I have been living life, bobbing & weaving my way through relationship after relationship and never taking a stand. Never being able to be knocked out and never being able to win. I have resisted against the things I have wanted and taken punishment for things that I have never sought. It's my no-win situation. My strategic defense of wearing down those that would seek me, by never fighting for them and never standing still long enough for them to grab hold of me. I have never been satis-fied because I have never chosen to fight for anyone that has chosen to love me.*

# AWAKENED

~

*I have walked blindly down the corridors of life hoping to find a treasure that I don't expect to find. Stumbling past support, friendship and love. I am blinded to reality and seek only those things I don't really need. I'm confused. I have no sense of direction. Living in places that offer me no future, no peace and no one to share my time with. My constant quest to get this or find that is what I live for. All love is questioned and I am unstable in where I am, my quest for a happy life. A life that allows me to relax and live just a little. To be able to love just a little or possibly find just a little bit of peace. To have the courage to chase happiness and expect to capture it. Shaking this fear I have of meeting the right woman or not letting go of the wrong woman. It forces me to sit at home day after day and miss out on all those things that I secretly want to find. It leaves me with unexciting days and uneventful nights. It creates a state of confusion, which leaves me puzzled in my understanding of what really makes me, me.*

*I have failed to understand my life and I blame her absence for it. Mommy is gone and finding a new anchor is no longer possible. The rock, that once was, has gone home and I am left by myself to fend for myself. I have become the store keeper and the cook. Having to wear both hats but having no experience at doing either. My little boy has peeped out of the windows of my mind and is afraid of what he has seen. His view of the world scares him, so he questions all that he knows and fights to go back to the way things were. He yearns for the good old days. He yearns for the times when he rode on his mother's shoulders without any thoughts of holding on. His identity was hidden within her arms. His future was where she chose to be on that day or at that time. He realizes that he needs her more now then when he was a young boy. When he was five, any woman would do, but now and forever more, only she would do. The super woman that possessed super powers. The powers that are needed in his life today. He needs her ears, which are able to quiet the noise of failure. Her hugs which were are able to stop bullets, knives and poor decisions. But most of all her words are needed, which had the ability to heal, the ability to strengthen and the ability to end the war within himself and bring peace to his life. When the storms of life raged out of control, her presence alone created a sense of calm. It is in those moments that he finds himself in need of her the most.*

*The hidden parts of me have been searching for that golden arrow of life. That arrow that is shot through the center of your heart and claims all that you are. This loneliness that lives within me is cancerous. A disease that quiets the room when the room is crowded. It pushes me into feelings of emptiness when others around me are hoping to be the loud voice that my ears want to hear. The loud bang that somehow awakens me to life or the soft tap on the shoulder that would wake me from my dreams. But it's not the tap on my shoulder from those that exist in my life today that's needed. It's my mother's tap. A voice whispered into my mind from a place high above. Small, simple words that carry a large powerful message. These are the words that would give me pause. A new opportunity to try it another way, do it with a different attitude and encourage me to try again. To ignore the thoughts to quit or the ease of letting go. Words that impress upon me to fight to change. To do it a new way or think about it in a different light. Her words tell me it is my time to find joy. This is the day that I find the me that I am supposed to be. Today I win the fight that I have lost on every other occasion. It's my time and I have been awakened to be the man that I was dreamt to one day be.*

# CHAPTER IV

*Love does not always manifest itself in smiles & laughter*

**Women lie**
*A dog is a dog is a dog is a dog.*

**That trick**
*For I know that in me dwelleth no good thing.  Romans 7:18*

**Scars**
*Our past is never forgotten, it lives behind the shadows.*

**You**
*If it's only about you, no one else will be able to share in it.*

**Never again**
*When love is no longer free, everything else will be for sale.*

**A second chance**
*Had he known how bad he hurt you,*
*he would never have asked for a second chance.*

**Independent**
*When there's no one but you, you lose the ability to love.*

**I'm just not ready**
*Love does not end when the relationship is over.*

**The ultimate player**
*The one who loves the least, makes the rules.*

**Nobody**
*If the rules are not bent they will never change.*

**I remember**
*Once your heart is broken, love becomes a game.*

# WOMEN LIE

~

*I found out today that women lie. Sounds strange or is that no big surprise to you? If you're a woman hearing these words, you chuckle within yourself and think, really? But to me and to most men, that's strange. Now I'm not talking about the average woman or some ho on the street. I'm talking about my woman. That soft spoken woman. That woman that just wants to be loved and treated with respect. The God fearing woman. The woman that told you how bad her last man treated her and how she was faithful from beginning to end. That's the woman I'm talking about. The one that allows you to go through her phone or question her as to where she's been. The woman that opens up her emotions for you to see. The one that begs for your time and wants to spend every waking moment with you. She's the one that lied. The one that swears by love of Christ that her words are true. The one that cries when things aren't going so well. The heartfelt one. The one that's been a victim of infidelity and physical abuse. The one that tries to love you in spite of your faults. She gives you foot messages, keeps your nails groomed and is sure to have a hot bath ready when you get home. She's the one I'm referring to. She drives the second car, eats the small piece of chicken and gets the glass of cold water when you're thirsty. Her words are the words that have lied to me.*

*I have questioned many things for many reasons, but of her, it has never been a question. But then there was today. Today my world changed. My sense of trust changed. My trust wasn't abused because of the lies that I found out about. My trust was abused because the lies that I found out about were in effect for months. Months ago a stranger's words meant more to her then my words. A text message carried more weight than my eye contact and a soft explanation. My truth took a backseat to her understanding, so she called me a liar. I was reminded of this over and over again and her loyalty, to me, was put on a pedestal. Again and again, she refused to accept my words. She was convinced of my failure and only stayed around to dish out some "get back". But she had lied. She used her beliefs of my cheating to justify her actions and so she herself continued to lie. Her web was exposed today and she faced it without any feelings of hypocrisy. She found reasons to explain it and refused to just recognize it. Cold would be too warm in describing her demeanor. I've eaten ice before and this wasn't ice. The one I trusted the most, lied to me the most. The one that gave all women I've met hope, has now given all women I'll meet reasons to be cautious. My guarantee is gone and women that were once safe are now in danger.*

*I had thought that men were the ones that needed to be taught to be faithful. Believing that only women were rooted in something stronger then their hormones. That women were somehow immune to the temptations that men refuse to fight against. Or simply that men tend not to fight against it until they're old and grey. I had thought, that should I be faithful, that women, or any women, would be willing to accept me. That somehow my struggle would not be their struggle. I found out today that what used to sound strange to me is now no big surprise, because today I found out that women lie.*

# THAT TRICK

~

*I'm not sure I'm going to make it. I have come a good distance but no outcome is near. Writing is becoming more difficult because my hopes appear to be nothing more than a pipe dream. Half the time I'm pissed, while the other half, I have my head up. What should make me happy? I have everything, but what I really want. Why can't one female slip on a banana peel and slide in my direction. Just one. I can talk to five or six, but my dumb ass wants just one. And that's what so crazy, because when I meet one female, she immediately wants to become the queen of her own dreams. She wants to be treated this way, talked to that way. Be told how wonderful she is knowing full well, she's given nothing of herself that would cause any man to utter those words, "you're wonderful." I'm supposed to believe you're wonderful because all the nice stuff you show me. All the good stuff you talk to your girlfriends about then criticizes men for not putting your "good stuff" on a pedestal.*

*I've heard this victim routine all too many times. I've been hurt; I've been used, mistreated, just like every other person out there trying to make it. I need to respect you! You don't respect me. You look at me the same way you look at everybody else. Another dude trying to extort some coochie from you, using words and money. Why should I be me when all I'm ever given is some self-serving story about how nice you are and how the "trick" that exists in you has never seen the light of day. Somehow the trick in you slept though that time your man slept with your best friend. Somehow the trick in you was "missing in action" when that man destroyed your good credit. Who are you fooling? Spending hours on the phone trying to convince me that your bitterness doesn't exist. Like I'm some kind of convict trying to escape a maximum security prison. While the trick in you is the guard, standing on the guard tower holding a sniper rifle, waiting for a brotha to run.*

*Show me that bitter woman in you when you hold me on the phone all night trying to see how sensitive of a man I am. That part of your past that you have on temporary lockdown. I've seen the good supporter, the friend and the humble woman you claim to be. Show me the built-up hostility you're hiding from me. The pain that comes out when things don't sound right, when things don't look right. Show me the part of you that could press a key up against a brand new Cadillac and then dare your man to call the police. The angry part of you that would be willing to spend two days in county jail just to mess up your man's income. I'm tired of seeing the good stuff, the phony stuff, the stuff that everyone gets to see. I want to know how much of a trick I'm going to have to deal with should this thing between us not work out.*

*And I'm never fooled into believing a woman is innocent. She hides the trick in her. She holds it down like a swallow of liquor, grinding her teeth together to keep from spitting it in your face. But she doesn't start out this way. The early signs can be seen when deep down inside you look over at her and think, "It's not going to be easy to cut this bitter trick loose." She doesn't become a pain in the ass until she does something so crazy and stupid that you feel you need to walk up to her face and tell her she's crazy.*

*So, that's the trick that I'm talking about. And when she comes out, make sure you have all your stuff, a new job, a new address and legal zoom because bitter women don't fight fair, they fight to win. You see, I can love a woman and I can accept her trying to figure out who I am and what I'm all about. But what I really want to know, is about that trick in her that has come out from time to time to make things right. That's the trick I want to talk about and that's the trick I want to be able to love.*

# SCARS

~

*People never heal from their scars and they don't really learn from the mistakes that they have made. They tend to believe they are stronger because of their scars and that they are wiser once their scars have healed. They are not. They remain blind to the effects caused by the hurtful acts of others and this has impacted their thinking. Imagine being lied to and manipulated to the point of entertaining thoughts of physical assault, grand larceny or attempted murder. You don't learn from that and you don't become stronger because of it. What new wisdom can be gained from thoughts of hurting someone you once loved, someone you still love and someone who is still able to affect you? Your conversations with others continue to be affected. Your thoughts and your thought process continue to be impacted and your interactions with others have surely changed. There is no wisdom to be gained from the suffering that has occurred in a relationship.*

*People never heal from their scars. They only learn new ways to protect themselves. Ways to hide their emotions then refer to it as strength. They become instant authorities on relationships and how to read and watch the actions portrayed by others. They become rigid and inflexible, never being able to accept the better angles of another human being. I have seen this pain for myself. Wanting to love a woman that doesn't believe that the love I give, is really love. By her estimation, I am only a short-timer and will not be around for very long. I will somehow change how I act, stop loving her and eventually leave her. She refuses to accept my love for her as genuine, so she waits for the relationship to fail. Her heart won't allow her to hope for true love, let alone maintain it. She is convinced that a man is not capable of loving her like a man would love his own daughter. That this man, no, this stranger, who has known her for only a short time, would never be able to ease her pain and love her. Her scars are just too large and the patience that she once had, has been pushed aside and replaced with cynicism. She will never believe that his love can endure her insecurities and he will not stay around long enough to receive the love that he expects in return. She is no fool. So she waits for failure like a child waits on the rain to cease. Rain that reminds her of her misery and the reality that informs to others, that her wounds are still not healed.*

*People never heal from their scars. They cover them up or mask them behind the false changes in their lives. They isolate themselves to the point that they can no longer function well with others. They become dysfunctional in their understanding of relationships and therefore are unable to maintain healthy ones. They look for reasons to question it. Reasons to justify the narratives that have been constructed in their minds. Reasons that will prevent them from ever admitting that they have healed and that their scars are no longer visible. Their relationships will be in constant disarray. They will continue to say that their scars are the source of their strength and they will continue to believe that their wounds are healed. Others will tolerate them and their relationships will continue to fail. They will continue to cover their wounds and others will continue to be blamed for their scars. Their scars have never healed!*

# *you*

*I didn't know that it was all about you. That my wants were never to be considered, not to be looked at and not a part of the conversation. It was always about you. Making sure you were lifted up and put on a pedestal, then worshipped as if you were an actual queen. A kind of royalty with no official bloodline. Your attempts to understand me were only your attempts to see how much I would spoil you. You wanted nothing of me, but everything from me. It was always all about you, your plan, your rules, your way. After the last man failed to follow this schedule, you moved on to me. A man with the resources to buy your love. A man that would allow you to play the game your way, on your terms and by your timetable. I was never really a factor, only a pawn in your chess match. A match that allowed you to withhold your heart and your intimacy and still expect to receive everything I would give to you. What you have actually sought is not love and romance, you sought payment and queen-ship. You placed your finger on the scale and tipped it into your favor. All that I received was inequality and injustice.*

*You used your creative tongue to encourage me to give and give some more. You told me that that was how love and commitment was to be shown. I was to give to you all of my time as long as you were available to receive it. Grant you all of my attention to show you how you will be pampered. And of course, bestow to you all of my finances so that you will not have to regret giving anything should this plan of yours fail to proceed according to your desires. After all, you do have a pot of gold hidden between your legs and that's what me and every man is really after. Your plan was to use this gold to encourage men to jump through hoops. You demanded the driver's seat and had no sense of urgency to give me back what I had given you so consistently. You subconsciously believed that intimacy is something that would only benefit me; therefore I am the one that must do the work to get it. It was never about us, it has always been about you.*

*The wining and dining was never an option to you, it was a requirement. All of the things that you expected to get out of me were just a part of your greater plan. The plan to get as much as you can get before I would realize that I was getting nothing in return. Your plan was genius because it was never about us, it was always about you. Your concept of a relationship, of the courting period, of the getting to know each other phase, it is distorted. Use him, but tell him it's just two people getting to know each other. Fool him, but convince him that you're not about sex you're about love and romance. Mislead him, by making him think that you are and have been, sacrificing just as much as he has. I have been a foolish pawn in your chess match. Doing everything I can do to show you my sincerity. Pouring out all of my emotions and allowing my arms to drop by my side, just in the hopes of showing you that I would not defend myself. To stand defenseless and allow love to batter me to and fro. To give all the things that you have always wanted, only to later find out that they have never meant anything. That the love I have shown was never able to penetrate the mistakes that were made in your past. My love was never able to be the exception to the rules that you now live by. My love has never stood a chance in your life because it was always about you.*

*So what exactly do I have left to give, that I have not already given? I had opened me up only to find that what's within me had no effect on you. You knowing that my heart was true was not enough. You knowing that I have withheld nothing from you has not seemed to matter. And even knowing that the changes in my life were only done so that I could better fit into yours, this was not enough. You wanted your opinions to be considered and they were. You wanted your feelings to be appreciated, so I cherished them. My heart told me to love you but your words only required that you be spoiled. So it is clear to me that you and I never stood a chance because I mistakenly believed that it was about us, when all the while it had always been just about you.*

# NEVER AGAIN

~

*I met another one today. Sexy smile, sexy body with an attitude to match. Aggressive in every sense of the word. I sat in the bushes and listened to her curse a man out for just asking her where she was. She was walking to the bus stop and had no patience for a man that wanted a little booty but wasn't willing to give her a ride to get some weed. She was low on estrogen and high on testosterone. She talks just like a man. Bold, forceful and impatient. She wouldn't stand for being played again. "Money for Booty" was her motto. No pay, no play! Brash is how she talks to you and she never mixes words when she wants something. Right now is her timetable. If you got it and she wants it, she expects to get it. Say no to her just once and she'll say no time for you. No more wasting her time, no to your wasted words, never again.*

*Her body is nothing more than a carrot. She'll dangle it right in your face. She'll talk about how good it is and then tell you it's been untouched for months. Her lies are obvious. She dresses like a hoochie and talks like a hooker. It's her game and it's all she knows now. She found her pot of gold. A bargaining tool that allows her to talk however she wants, whenever she wants and to whomever she wants. Question her, then forget you. The last ten men that lied to get some of her gold changed her. Somehow destroyed what was left of her femininity. They crushed her hope in men and her belief in honesty. They were not your average players. They were players of the game. Old school balers that expected to give up a little money from time to time. The game was to get the gold and giving up a few "C" notes was just a part of it. She alone was the victim, but never again.*

*Her trust had been broken. She had nothing left in her that wasn't already taken, used or abused. She was cursed with a sexy body and men were never able to see the insecure little girl that was hidden behind her smile. All that was left in her was anger, hurt and pain. She was broken. A victim of giving too much, way too soon. Her treasure was taken from her and all the remained was her coochie. This tool that unknowingly caused man after man to use her over and over again. She never realized its effects on men. She was thinking love and romance and men were thinking coochie and more coochie. She finally realized that it was never about her. It was never about a relationship. Her feelings were stepped on, her trust was destroyed and she was left alone, humiliated and helpless, but never again.*

*Never will she allow another man to control the conversation or orchestrate the program. It's her show now. Her rules. Her way! "You want some coochie ...well, whatcha got for me? Sister got bills...so what you trying to do?" That was her slogan. Her theme song that now plays in the back of her mind. The only tune that she would listen to. Her "little black book" that would allow her to be the player and not the played. Try to tell a joke to make her smile, "Sister got bills!" Spot her twenty dollars to get some weed, "Whatcha tryin to do?" She's hip to the game now. Word's don't mean anything if that's all you plan on giving her. She knows what you want and what you'll do to get it. So she works you over, like a boxer works a heavy bag. Punch, punch, punch, bob-n-weave. Punch, punch, punch, bob-n-weave. She knows that if she offers you the gold, you'll take it. Then couldn't even tell her what her last name is. You're the same as the last loser, Loser! So she will never allow herself to be hurt again. She's wide awake now and the game that's being played is hers. No more tricks with your sensitive words and you're laid back demeanor. No more games without giving a little money and a little time. And no more lies about what it is you're really after. So, coochie for free, never again!*

# A SECOND CHANCE

~

*I don't deserve it. It's not wise to give it to me and I'm not entirely sure I can even handle it. A second chance. A chance to do the things I promised to do the first time. A chance to mend the broken pieces that were shattered by my lies. A chance to speak plainly when words need not be spoken. A deja vu of the relationship. A second chance to fill the potholes in the relationship. Holes dug when you were not in my presence and my insecurities caused me to be the man I promised to never be. That player that stepped out on your loyalty. The baller that gave your love to another woman. The gift of a second chance, to me, it's not deserved.*

*A second chance? How about no chance. How about a chance to allow him to get his shit before his shit gets burnt. A chance to get his car before his car gets towed. He says he's different now. He's changed. Snakes change. They shed their skin ever so often, but a snake is still a snake is still a snake. So take this chance to find your way out. Use this time to find the man that was "missing in action" when she needed a friend. Find that communicator you claimed to be, that left her hanging when she needed someone to talk to. Take all the time you need because your time is no longer needed in her life. Your future attempts to hit it again and again and then find an excuse to leave again will be met with disgust.*

*She will forever remember your sea of lies and deceit and wanting only a little coochie from time to time, but not being man enough to simply say that. A second chance. To a man, it's nothing more than another opportunity for him to give absolutely nothing, but expect everything. Your games are over. Your request for a second chance is denied! You pleas for a do-over are rejected! Blame your mistakes on your past, on your hormones or on your ignorance. Those apologies, the flowers and the new promises no longer have the effect they once had. You've had your second chances again and again. The words you need to deal with now are "never again." Maybe your friends can explain them to you. Maybe you've heard them the last time you played your games. But you can be sure you won't be given an opportunity to recover from these mistakes. Your kissing her again will be only a fantasy. Your touching her again will only be a dream that will surely end. Your pleas for a second chance have fell on death ears. And if you wonder if that will every change, the answer is "hell no."*

# *INDEPENDENT*

~

*I met a woman today that sparked thoughts of marriage. She flashed a winning smile, a creative conversation and a sense of humor that made me laugh. Her body was not a dime but it was much more then the nickel that I have been carrying around for myself. She wore a physique that I would be proud to walk beside. Chocolate skin, painted nails and a look that took her longer than ten minutes to make right. This was it. The right one at the right time saying the right things. She wore her independence on her sleeve and she wasn't afraid to show it. Paying her own bills, her own way, with her own money. No help from baby daddies. No help from mom or dad and no help from the State. Together. That's what her friends called her. She's on point with hers and always seems to get things done. A soldier among women, who only seek the emotions of men and not what men can buy her. She spoke words plainly and expected plain answers in return. She lives by her motto of "know what you know and don't be afraid to speak it."*

*I met a woman today that sparked thoughts of marriage. She wears her emotions like she wears the necklace that hangs around her neck. Just above her shoulders and close to her heart. Like her necklace, you see her emotions long before you confront her. She speaks thoughts that are not always appropriate to speak and it reveals how she feels long before your ready to hear them. Early thoughts that are typically never told. Thoughts that reveal her intentions and highlight her fears. She is an emotional roller-coaster that searches for a man that will allow himself to scream and be heard screaming. A man that will raise his arms high and allow the sinking feelings to overtake him. Someone that will let go of that thing that holds him back from loving, only to join hands with her so that they may fall in love together.*

*I met a woman today that sparked thoughts of marriage. She is very aware of her imperfections. Her largest character flaw being her inability to resist intimacy. Having no capacity to ration it and hoping only that what she gives is what he wants. Speaking openly about her likes and dislikes and she is yet to meet a man that she is unable to please. She continues to give too much of what she has and gets too little of what she wants. She is insatiable and she knows it. Limited by her morals of wanting the comfort of just one man. A man able to measure up to her every expectation. One that is able to handle the workload that he will be given, both physically and emotionally. She wants a lover and a friend, a husband and a father, a thinker and a comedian. She wants it all and nothing short of that will be acceptable. She will not accept anything less than 100 percent. He must measure up to all of her hopes because she is determined to reject any effort to give her anything less. She will refuse to compromise her hopes and in doing so she will never meet a man worthy of her full love and attention. She will search for something never to be found and complain about something she will never be able to receive. She will find it difficult to meet someone that she can love and that someone that can love her, will only ever meet her dream of loving someone else.*

# THE ULTIMATE PLAYER

~

*You'll find her sitting at the bar waiting patiently for the game to begin. This is her environment, but on her last hunt she failed to capture what her appetite was so hungry for. She patiently eyes the terrain as she baits her hook. Other players of her caliber use smiles, conversations and their looks to bait their hooks. She uses coochie. The possibility of it, the chance you may see it, the hopes you may rub up against it. She doesn't normally use coochie as her bait because it always puts her prey in a frenzy. But today, she wants the big catch. She's like a single lioness trying to take down a cape buffalo; it's never been done. Under normal circumstances it would take several lions working in unison over a reasonable period of time to take down a cape buffalo. Experience has taught her that you can bite him until he bleeds, you can scratch him and claw at him, but he's too damn strong. His employment is stable, his status is professional and the 401K that he tells you about has been in effect for years. You can see his strength from a distance. He strolls around not bothering to look up to watch for approaching predators. There are many. Even when you get close to him, he drives you around the city in a nice car, two movies, a dinner a Ruth's Chris, a new outfit and this player, I mean this cape buffalo doesn't have a scratch on him.*

*She convinces herself that she is willing to risk life and limb, because she wants her cape buffalo and she doesn't want to share him. She knows his weak spot though, his throat. She has to get her teeth around his throat and hold it long enough to take him down. She knows she can't take him down with the typical bait, so baiting her hook with coochie is her only option. She has nothing else strong enough to bring him to his knees. Nothing else can get him low enough so that she can get her teeth around his throat. She sees the old scars across his torso and knows that coochie may have been tried before, but failed. She had to believe that her coochie was different, it was wetter, softer and she wasn't beyond using all of her lips to get her cape buffalo down. Memories of her last attempt to take down a cape buffalo are still fresh in her mind. She is reminded of her failure daily, as she prepares her son to enter kindergarten. Since that time she has had a many sleepless nights trying to figure out why she failed. It wasn't until recently she* *came to understand, that it wasn't enough to just get her teeth around his neck, she needed strong claws, a strong back and she had to be in shape. She also realized that she could not allow herself to be turned into the prey. With that in mind, she was sure to take care of her own hunger in the privacy of her shower. She sharpened her claws down at the Chinese nail salon, she called her girlfriend over to get her hair done and she strengthened her backside with the pair of $200 apple bottom jeans she would wear the day of.*

*She was ready. The game was on. Now, she had to lure her cape buffalo from his grazing area to an area that would give her one-on-one access. She decided to spread her scent so she accidentally dropped her cell phone, bent over to pick it up and without missing a beat, she walked away. He caught her scent immediately. Her back could feel his eyes following her across the room, desperately hoping he could make eye contact. She sat and turned into his direction giving him exactly what he wanted. An opportunity. He began to throw game at her to see what would stick. It was like he was shaking his manhood after a long piss. She wanted him to shake in until he turned himself on. He shook and shook, but what came out was not what she had expected. The Cape buffalo had evolved. He began shaking out poetry, understanding and his desire to be monogamist. He shook it out and allowed it to drip into her mind. She felt a tingling sensation and began to jiggle. It was her that was on the hook. It was no longer his throat she wanted. This lioness had realized that one coochie was not enough to take a real player, I mean, a cape buffalo down.*

# NOBODY

~

*Nobody really loves me. Those that have access to me don't want who I am and those that want me, hide what their after. I'm not a prize, I'm fool's gold. I'm shiny, desired and I have great characteristics, but I'm not valuable. I'm a gift with nothing inside. You're excited for a while and disappointed the rest of the time. Like this gift, I am empty inside, but it's not due to a lack of substance, my silence, or my failure to give. It's due to me not accepting the rules that others live by. It's me not agreeing with what others presume to be normal or appropriate. It's my resistance to the way things are.*

*I have given up on finding happiness in a woman. Not because it's not in women, but instead, because women of a certain age, no longer give. Because of their past failures, they now want to be chased, courted, pursed and dated. The very things they were given when they were teenagers. That love that was shown through the small priceless nibblets of life we refer to as "puppy love". It is this past that is sought by the rejected, the humiliated, by women. The events in life have conditioned them this way. It has caused them to be guided by history and tradition. How men are to give, how men are to love and how men are to interact with women. If a man says, "Let's go to the movies", it means he should pick you up, pay for the movie tickets and buy the popcorn. His suggestion is somehow translated into something that he never intended it to be, yet women continue to seek a man that believes that this is what a man is supposed to do. They also believe that a man, a good man, should be sensitive, loving and giving. This is reasonable; however, they fail to list the items that a woman should do. After being hurt, women seek nothing less then everything. They expect to be dated for months with no expectation of intimacy. They expect a man to give everything, both financially and emotionally, while they themselves give absolutely nothing. They see themselves as the prize, their bodies as a temple and their love as a trophy. They seek only the potential of a man and not the substance found within him. A substance that they never get to see because of their insistence on seeing his potential only. So a woman's hope can be likened to that of a hot-air balloon. It's capable of flying, but it can only go so high before its potential to go higher is exhausted.*

*Nobody really loves me. Not the readers of these words and not those that claimed to have loved me in times past. Everyone has conditions, rules and barriers to which, they will not cross. I am alone and I sit alone. Only my potential is loved. Only my perspective is loved. Only my thought process is loved. This stringing together of adjectives and verbs are loved and it is these things that seem to bring a sense of value to me. Even so, none of these things am I able to bottle up and hand to another person. None of these things am I able to produce in abundance to purchase tickets to see a movie. None of these things am I able to barter with, which would allow me to take someone on a cruise of some sort. All of the potential I am thought to have is not able to buy anything tangible to show her love. It is my words without works, my wisdom without movement or my potential never to be realized. It is the packaging around me only, a form of fool's gold that is not able to be used to purchase anything of value. It serves only as a temporary happiness that is sure to end. The fuel to an automobile or the fork for a meal. It is the frosting that women seek to see in men. A frosting which could never sustain them, but is still needed because they need to be fooled. Their past heartbreak makes them this way. Their need for glitz in a relationship to encourage them to trust again. It is this fool's gold that is sought from me by women, which tell me that nobody really loves the real me. Nobody.*

# I REMEMBER

I remember when holding back my feelings was not even a thought. When my love for you was never questioned. When giving all of me and all that I have access to was the norm. I remember when kissing made me laugh and holding hands made me proud. When all of my love letters began with, "I love you" and ended with "You and I, forever." I remember when we calculated our last names so that they added up to marriage. When calling you was not just all that time, it was for all of my time.

I remember when sex was never in our conversations, but grinding was our thing. When going to the movies was as simple as saying "hello" because it didn't matter what was playing or who was playing in it. I remember when chasing you around a parked car was just as magical as sitting with you at Mickey D's. I remember when we went everywhere together and did everything together. When buying you the perfect Christmas gift caused me to sweat when you opened it. When I wrote you little notes throughout the day and hid them in places you would find them. I remember picking out our kid's names and spots on the map that we would visit one day. I remember when being attracted to another girl was never a temptation for me. When dating you forever seemed logical and anything less was unacceptable. I remember when having you wear my football jersey showed our friends that we belonged to each other. When that plastic ring I got you from the gum ball machine meant much more than the 25 cents I spent to get it. When your name was scribbled in my every text book and your smile was visible in my every memory. I remember when being told that I was "whipped" was not an issue and I didn't even understand what it meant anyway. I remember when our arguments caused me to stay up nights and our breakups only served to remind us of how much we liked each other. I remember.

But I also remember when our argument lasted a day too long and our immaturity caused our egos to guide us. When "we" ended and "you and I" began. When my anger overruled my love for you and I suffered my first heartbreak. Those memories have since faded and I now remember only questioning every girl's motives and every girl's love. I now remember never being able to laugh without *being suspicious. Never being able to love without worrying about being hurt. I now remember giving only enough to get what I wanted. Never taking walks in the park again. Never sitting together and cuddling to watch our favorite shows together. Never giving our best to each other. Never listening with understanding to each other and never again accepting the best from each other. I now remember dating other girls just in case you and I didn't make it. Never giving you a fair chance to show me how much you loved me. Never trusting your words, your actions or even your emotions. Never allowing you to get a piece of the real me. The piece that is hidden behind my deep voice, my clever words or my phony smile. I now remember never opening up to you and sharing my day with you. Never believing that you and I would last forever, only preparing for you and I to fail together. I now remember hurting you in ways that I was hurt. Never admitting that I was wrong and never telling you the full truth. Never allowing you to meet my family, visit my home town or go on vacations with me. Never opening my life to you, my heart to you and sharing my fears with you. I now remember that I no longer remember.*

# CHAPTER V

*Giving up is not an option, if moving on is still possible*

### I'm just not ready
*As long as he's chasing a ghost, he will never be able to catch you*

### She says she's not the one
*Know thyself and accept that which is known to you.*

### Victory
*It's not always what it seems.*

### Don't change
*All change is not good.*

### Courage
*It is the key ingredient to living a successful life.*

### It's my fault
*Insecurity is not a characteristic,*
*it's the byproduct of a failed relationship.*

### Men feel it too
*Failed relationships affect men and women alike.*

### I'm that man
*Men are not the only ones that fail to see the forest for the trees.*

### Tears
*Live life through the trials of others, not just your own.*

### Never settle
*Life is more about the walk and less about the arrival*

### Sacrifice
*You can't let go, if you're still holding on.*

# I'M JUST NOT READY

~

*I'm not ready to be the man that I said that I am. I was mistaken when I told you that you were the one I wanted. I misspoke when I mentioned to you that I am ready to love you to my fullest. I'm just not ready.*

*Not because you're not what I have waited for. In fact, you're everything that I have waited for. You are more than I have expected, but I'm still not ready. I am just not able to love you unconditionally. I can love you; I just don't believe I am able to stop loving her. That other girl; the one that has caused so much havoc in my life. Her, the very woman that I told you I didn't care about. The woman that toyed with me like a newborn baby and walked away from me when I was drowning. Her, I am not ready because I am not able to stop loving her, the one that hurt me. My past reminds me of her and of what women are capable of. And because of that, my present should tell you exactly what men are not capable of. Dysfunctional would be an understatement, so forgive me. Your soft touch is everything I need, but I'm not capable of relaxing when you touch me. Your understanding is what encourages me to tell you the truth, but I just don't seem to want to speak when I'm around you. Your love for me is without question. If I had any doubt of that, I would tell you so. And it's not because your love is too much for me, I'm just not ready.*

*If you're wondering why I still love her, then so am I. If I could explain my stupidity, we would already be married. So, I find myself wrestling with the thought of asking you to wait on something to change within me? Do I caution you that this situation has been in play for some time now? It has never changed from the way it has been and I've tried. Time and time again I have wanted to love you, but time and time again, I have chosen not to love. Not to give of myself which would have been a fitting response to the love and attention that you have shown me. So time and time again it is clear, I have failed. I have failed to love you back. And time and time again that voice in you has come to the same conclusion that I have come to, I'm just not ready.*

*I wish I could tell you that I just want to sleep around. That I simply want variety in my life and that the dog in me just wants to bark, but I cannot. I do only want just one woman, it's just that the woman that I want was created from the rib of a man whose name was Adam. You can't compete with that. So maybe when I'm an old man long past my fertile years, I will be able to love you in an appropriate way. But as for today, I'm just not ready.*

# SHE SAYS SHE'S NOT THE ONE

~

*She's not that event my heart has been waiting for. She's says she's only a placeholder. Someone here today, just for today. Her arrival should not be announced to the masses. She has no royal blood running through her veins. There is no special beauty that she alone poses. So she says she's not the one.*

*Her smiles over the phone and via text messages are of no real importance. Her desires to love a good man are no more surprising then the rising of the sun. She needs him like she needs air to breathe. She's incomplete without him. She's incomplete without someone to grow old with. But she says she's not the one.*

*She looks within herself and sees no special mixture. She believes there are no combination of qualities within her that could be twisted or measured in such a way as to give her an advantage over another woman. She simply relaxes in who she believes she is to be. A superwoman in her own mind, never competing to be any more or any less then who she is. If competition is what's required, she's chooses to be last because she chooses not to compete. She's on a list all by herself. One woman, one lover, one friend, just one man. But she says she's not the one.*

*She listens to others as they fight to make sense of their misery. She listens to the stories of failed relationships, family issues and failures in life. She is a counselor with no degree to speak of. She secretly waits for her turn to lay on the therapy couch. To be given her opportunity to tell her story. A victim herself, due to her failure to love just a little, but instead, she loved too much. She failed to trust just a little, and instead, trusted everyone way too much. She wanted to give just a little, but instead, ended up giving 120 percent. So she has no advice for other. She simply extends her ability to just listen. Responding only with a node, a smile and a "girl it's gonna to be ok." Who is she to speak when she herself refuses to give up hope. She refuses to not hope for that fairytale relationship that continues to be just a fairy tale. But she says she's not the one.*

*She says she's not the supportive friend or that loving partner. She says she only loves to the fullest and expects simply to be loved back. She only loves first, second and last. She does not expect things that she has not already given herself. Her specialty is who she is, her beauty is what you feel and her love is what she gives. She has failed on every occasion, on her every attempt and in every relationship she has been a part of. This is why she says she's not the one.*

# VICTORY

*I can see victory from here. I had been standing here for quite a while but was facing the wrong direction. I thought I was moving toward it. I thought it would be found down the path that I had chosen. It was not. I had been walking the road of destruction. A road paved with money, women and power. The glare of the bright lights had dazzled me. The pretty smiles and all of the expensive things seem to have distracted me. It was exactly what I had been conditioned to want. Those things that society told me success was to be. I wanted it all. My choice was made based on the lies that I was led to believe. Lies told to me by family, friends and strangers. Generational lies that each of us must fight against. Generational lies that each of us has failed against.*

*I can see victory from here. Just around the corner, over the bend and across the river. My vision was obstructed by my ego. It had grown at the same rate as my income. They went hand in hand. I thought I would always stay the same. That I would remain grounded throughout my life. That the once broke me, would act just like the big money me. But I changed and I had convinced myself that my actions would be the same with or without rent being paid. That my swagger would look identical whether or not I drove a Lexus or caught the bus. I had lied to myself and all those around me only helped to perpetuate that lie. Maybe even to the point that I cannot not change back. Back to the point when "hello", trumped "hey baby" and "how are you doing" carried more weight than "what's up." I have changed and it worries me that there may not be enough of the old me left around, to force the new me to change back.*

*I can see victory from here. I had been looking for something shiny, something cute and something that others would see as valuable. My victory was close so I made plans to meet it. I did not find victory, but victory somehow found me. It was more than I expected but not what I had imagined it to be. It was not gold and its' worth could not be purchased. It was as bright as the shining sun but it somehow only blinded me. It had been there all along waiting for me to change. For me to change directions, to change my attitude and to change what I had always believed victory to* be. *I could not find this victory because I could not turn the corner, I was unable to go around the bend and I had no means of crossing the river. So I could not find my victory, but yet my victory somehow found me. She had traveled a great distance, for a long time and now I can see my victory and my victory can now see me.*

# DON'T CHANGE

~

*Don't change that pleasant smile or that loving spirit that can brighten a dull day. Don't change your soft touch or the way you massage my shoulders when I'm tired. Don't change the way you look at me when I'm trying to impress you. I need it. I know I don't tell you I do, but I love it. But even without that, don't change.*

*I have been nothing short of unpredictable. I have failed to communicate. I have put your emotions on hold and I continue to give you reasons to question my motives, but don't change. Don't change your ability to be forgiving or your decision to forgive my failures; it's a treasure to me. Your calls to say hello and your text messages lets me know that you're thinking of me. Those smiles and that constant quest to get more time in my life is what I have always wanted, so don't change. Overlook my lack of time for you and my failure to make room for you in my life, it's only temporary. Keep giving your all, there's no need to stop doing that. Keep believing in the man that I am not, I'll come around. I can't tell you when or even if it will be worth your wait, but know that I will appreciate it. I may just surprise you, so don't change.*

*Don't change the way you accept my flaws or the way you support me when I am in the wrong. Don't change that. I know that I have never appreciated a good woman. I've never fought to save a good relationship and I've never stayed around long enough to get through the learning period. I have been long on rules and short on patience. I have tried to read books to understand my insecurities, but I have been unable to finish them. They seem to be written with a spirit of compromise, a quality that I am short on. They required me to see myself through your eyes, from your perspective. To view me without my ego, my pride and this fear I have of loving a woman back. I have never finished that book, so I still don't know much about women, but even so, please don't change. Call upon your ability to tolerate unfairness and imbalance in a relationship. You have used those powers before in the past, so don't change that now. Fight for me even when I refuse to fight for you, so don't change.*

*But if your heart tells you to change all that, then cut me loose quickly. Give me no possibility of a do over and don't allow me to* come back when your memory of my mistakes has faded. I do apologize for wasting any of your time or hurting your feelings in any way. I can't imagine how hard it's been for you. I can see why you may consider changing your ways in the future. But don't be so quick to do that. Don't be so quick to adjust those parts of you that have given me the most joy. Be careful changing that. But if you must change, change your selection criteria for finding a good man only. Because those things that you have given me are and will always be, priceless. It is in reference to these things that I respectively advise you on behalf of myself and men every-where...don't change.

# COURAGE

~

*It is the willingness to fail. The possibility that you're best will fall short. The knowledge that your inadequacies will be exposed. It is the ability to move forward in the face of an unknown outcome. Courage. It is sometimes referred to as "guts" or "gall" and when applied to certain situations, it will force one to come face to face with ones' fears. Internal fears. Fears that others may be able to face, but fears you may have run from for a lifetime. It is not something that can be overcome with ease, so it can never be mastered. It never gets old and it never runs out. It is available to you every day and in every situation. It's not isolated to the strong, the fit or the intellectual. It hides within each of us and each of us has the ability to produce it. Not everyone has common sense, but everyone has within themselves the capacity to demonstrate courage.*

*We sometimes show courage and mask it behind circumstances, luck, coincidence or happenstance. Courage is not bright. It's not easily seen, but even in the dark or in dark situations, courage can reveal itself. Sometimes it can only be recognized by others. In those moments when a victim of abuse says, "Stop. Stop hurting me. Stop using me." When one says enough is enough. When you've taken all you can take and your mind says, "no more." That's courage. It forces you to go against what you have been accustomed to. To go against the advice of a close friend even when they have your best interests at heart. Your friends sometime encourage you to do this or to do that, knowing full well that their words will be of little comfort should you move outside of your comfort-zone. These friends tend to advise you to take a stand. And in doing so, your willingness to act after having been motionless, or your ability to speak after finding yourself speechless, this is called courage.*

*It's gasoline to an automobile, legs to the marathon runner and a good book to the avid reader. It is what enables each of us to fight for what we believe in. It is what makes the lied-to trust again, the broken hearted love again and the fearful face failure once again. The abused says, "No more." The drug-user, says "never again" and the lonely searches for a crowd. Courage. To face the shortfalls of life and show the willingness to resist against them. To risk starting over with nothing more than a hope and a prayer.*

*It's the bright light that shines on our private mistakes. It's the voice of reason when our ability to listen has failed us. It is our strength when everything about our situation encourages us to give up. It is bundled within our makeup and has proven itself to be a quality that lives within each of us, but a quality that each of us on occasion, refuses to let live. Courage.*

# IT'S MY FAULT

~

*The way you question me on where I've been or what I've been doing. The way you ask question after question just to be clear about my not-so-clear answers. Never wanting to seem insecure, only looking for a way to trust me again. The way you fight day after day not to go through my phone or ease-drop on my conversations. Your struggle to accept the notion that men do sometimes change. As for the reasons why you do that, it's my fault; I caused you to be this way.*

*The way you walk slowly around me and talk softly when we argue. The way you're careful about how you speak to me to keep my temper from rising. You ability to speak softly when your heart tells you to scream. Holding firm to your hopes of receiving the better side of me, even if it's only for short time. And the way you accept my logic when everything in you has rejected my logic. The way you show up when I need you to be there. The way you speak up when I need you to be heard. As for the reasons why you do that, it's my fault; I caused you to be this way.*

*The way you listen to me when I talk for hours, just to encourage me to listen to you just for a moment. Fighting that emotional fight with me to hear of the soft man that seems to be locked away somewhere. Hoping daily that something will change in me, or just maybe a bell will ring within my soul that will wake me up to your love for me. The way you search my soul looking for the great man within, then anxiously wait for him to step forward. Showing patience when you want to push and showing restraint when your hands want to grab. The way you touch me without using your hands and tell me you love me without using your lips. As for the reasons why you do that, it's my fault; I caused you to be this way.*

*The way you plan events for us to attend only to have me back out again and again. Encouraging me to go to different places, only to find yourself alone in those different places. The way you make plans for family and kids alone, planning vacations alone and feeling that you're in the relationship alone. The way you always make room for the things in my life, but never having room be made for you in my life. The way you send signals to me to talk to you, hoping simply to get a small piece of me. As for the reasons why you do that, it's my fault; I caused you to be this way.*

*I am to blame for your walking around on eggshells. I am to blame for your insecurities that never before existed. If not for your love for me, you would have been gone long ago. I can only imagine that you're still here because you still love me. Because you still believe there's hope for me. Because you still believe in pig tails and fairy tales. Because you know you're doing everything you can to make it work and should we fail, you will find comfort in knowing... it's my fault, I caused you to be that way.*

# MEN FEEL IT TOO

*She has always felt that way. She will never find what she's look-ing for and she will never be able to recognize that all men are not dogs. Her feeling that I am not romantic enough or that I only want sex from her. Her decision to not argue with me because she feels she shouldn't have to walk on eggshells when she speaks. Her belief that she has no room in her mind for disagreement. She knows what she knows and her instincts tell her that no man, not even a loving man, can tell her anything new about how men func-tion. She's cynical, she never expects relationships to last. She tries anyway, rooted in her belief that every man should be treated equally. That no man deserves to be punished based on the sins of another man. That was her theme song, but her actions never played that tune. She was lip-syncing because her guards where never completely let down.*

*To hear her tell it now, she was testing me. Her plan was to use lit-tle words and creative catch phrases that would give her the infor-mation she needed to determine if I am the man in her fairy tales. She had failed to find him all of her life and didn't really expect to find him in me. I just had a few of the right qualities that she felt she deserved. She thought maybe if she coupled that with her great sex and her financial independence, she could probably come close to building the man that she wanted. Maybe mold me into the man that she has dreamt about. It was genius. She had come up with a scenario that would allow her to get everything she wanted with-out risking the things she had always risked before.*

*But it was not to be. I found this out today, but wish I had known that she had always felt that way. The way she rewrote history after every argument. The way she reads the tea leaves even though the leaves where made of plastic. She could come up with a cause to fit any situation and she did it without even considering who I am. My character, in her mind, deserved no consideration. My status, my logic, my style were just pawns that all men used to get what they wanted. She was exceptional with how she used innocent words to poke at me. Words she disguised behind smiles, laughter and sarcasm. Saying something insulting about who I am then telling me, not to get my panties in a bunch. "I'm just kidding* boo" was her anthem. She found reason after reason to explain to herself what I think or why I think what I think. Me telling her what I think was nothing more than a creative falsehood, commonly known as a lie. She was never wrong in her analysis, so even when she explained it to me, it was my failure to understand that caused confusion. I'm a man and I'd have to be a woman to understand how to interpret her gibberish. I was to blame for her inability to articulate what she thought about this or how she felt about that. I'm just a man so my logic would not allow me to ignore facts in order to comprehend her reasoning.

I can imagine her now talking with her girlfriend explaining to her how she saw it all along. How she had a feeling about this or that for some time now. She'll talk her way into believing that her initial instincts were correct. She will create her own little narrative to explain away her every position. She'll be able to explain to her girlfriend all her little tale-tell signs of a troubled relationship. She'll do it without one piece of blame being placed on her actions. She will paint herself as the innocent participant that was being bullied by the big bad man. Without even knowing it, she will clone herself within the mind of her girlfriend. And her girlfriend will become another disgruntle female that evaluates a man's character based solely on whether or not the relationship lasts. Excuse my characterization of her, it's not based in fact. It's only a reflection of my anger at her and the pain I feel at losing someone that I care about. She's not a disgruntle female. She's just another trick that's made my skin crawl after trying my best to treat her with respect and honesty. But she's not a trick either. She's just a bitter woman that has an axe to grind with any and every man that she will ever meet. She will never find what she's looking for and she will never be able to recognize that all men are not dogs, some of us have feelings too.

# I'M THAT MAN

~

*All of the prayers that appear to have been unanswered. The fasting, the praying and the commitments that you have made in secret. The preparations that you seem to have made room for in your life. Your schedule, having changed it to fit that new thing that you are preparing for. Your routine, which has expanded to include daily walks, workouts and healthy eating. All of the adjustments that have been made, just to make room. Room for an acceptable counterpart in your life. I'm that man.*

*The burying of past mistakes, past relationships and past decisions. The releasing of the old ways things were done in your past. Accepting less then what you have deserved and giving more than you ever should have. Never weighing his words against his actions, but instead, hoping his actions could live up to your words. The phone calls that you expected to continue and never cease. The walks in the park that would show his commitment to quality time in the relationship. Evaluating him according to your needs and not based on your unrealistic expectations. Your simple needs, your basic wants and your heartfelt desires. Placing him alongside you and not in front of you. Being his springboard to bounce ideas off of and not a board to be walked upon. Searching for places and events you will one day visit together. Holding his hand in crowded rooms and kissing him softly in public places. You imagine the thrill of staring into each other's eyes just to say "I love you." You do this innocently, all in the hopes of doing it the right way this time. Trusting him with the right mindset and loving him before others are willing to even accept him. You openly risk anything just for a chance to receive everything. You see now what others have yet to see. I'm that man.*

*You adjust your conversations to make them informative and well above all sexual overtones. Never accepting less than full commitment and full respect from him. Preparing your closest friends and all of your family members for his pending arrival. His arrival in their lives and the realization of his position in yours. The protector of your heart and the beneficiary of your dreams. He is worth it because you have already seen the blueprint that he was created from. Discussing the type of work he does with friends. How he raises his kids and his relationship with his mother. You have already listened to his thoughts and supported him in his endeavors. Watching him from a distance, knowing that he will be the man that you believe him to be. The way he holds you when you walk beside him. The way he makes you laugh when there is no laughter in you. His normal has you doing jumping jacks and his abnormal makes you speak of marriage. I'm that man.*

*You have found that his touch is able to invoke changes in your outward as well as your inward presence. The sound of his voice makes you want to cuddle and his thought process makes you want to close your eyes and enjoy the music. He is what you have been waiting for and he does not fade away when he is pinched. You have found him in your today and he has asked to love you throughout your tomorrows. Words that you have been wanting to hear, coming from the man that you are waiting to love. You tell everyone you know that you are now taken, because within the fabric of your being you believe him to be that man. The man that your heart has waited for is that man you believe God has created for you. I'm that man.*

# TEARS

~

*I have found tears, not my tears, the tears delivered by life. The pain of accepting the death of a loved one. The heartbreak of a failed relationship. The disappointment of a child that has failed to heed their parent's scolding. Life's tears.*

*My tears are not for me. There for the pains that life brings to each of us. Sometimes the pain of a broken leg causes us tears. Sometimes it's the joy of a wedding or the arrival of a child. Life causes us tears and life has the ability to dry them up. Within each of us there can be found the catalyst for tears. The things that have truly shaped us. Many tend to believe that your actions clearly reveal these items. That a strong man is affected more by the affliction of a child rather then the joy of a wedding. We associate strong things to men and emotional things to women. Even I have fallen in line to this sort of thinking. I have never cried at a wedding, the birth of one of my children or the breaking of my wrist when I was a young boy. I was never taught not to cry, I was just never shown how to cry. How to look at an event or situation and have empathy for those that were involved. Who teaches that?*

*My tears are not for me. There for all of the situations that warrants tears. Situations that are not simply related to the painful things in life. Situations that have a powerful affect on the masses or situations that we feel it's appropriate to cry in. Our tears should not be limited to that. They should be available in our daily actions. Knowing that we are loved, the appreciation of the kindness of others or seeing a homeless man asking for some change. We fail to shed life's tears, because we fail to see life through the eyes of others. Imagine for a moment not having food, clothing or a place to live. Imagine for a moment losing mom, dad, siblings and children. Imagine an accident causing you to lose the use of your legs or your vision or even your ability to speak. Our tears are in silence, so we casually empathize with the situation but never appreciate it. We call it "that" or "them". We patronize them, say that we understand and we are sympathetic in how we deal with them. This is not empathy. Empathy requires us to hate the unfairness of society. To become our brother's keeper. To seek to help all those, rich or poor, with the pains of life. Our income levels do not dictate our pain level. Yes, our pains are different but all of us will experience life's punches in one fashion or another. It is from these burses that our characters are shaped, our thoughts are established and our opinions are sharpened.*

*My tears are not for me. It for the man that does not have what I have, the family that lives from paycheck to paycheck or the multi-millionaire that just lost his son. It is to these that I lend my tears. It is to these that I pray for. I am thankful for all that I have stewardship over. I am thankful that I have a sound mind and a healthy body. My tears are not for me. There for my brothers and my sisters in life. I feel your pains and I cry with you. Knowing your pains causes my tears to flow, so my life is no longer just about me, it's about the tears that now run down my eyes, but these tears are not for me.*

# SACRIFICE

*I'm not as hard as I seem to be. My silence is not due to my lack of having something to say. The disagreements that we have is uncomfortable to me as much as it is to you. But I'm not yet ready to throw in the towel.*

*I'm not entirely sure how to love you because I am not yet able to function in a fluid fashion emotionally. These mechanical actions that you see, are my attempts to be the man that my heart tells me I am. There are no instinctive feelings I can boast about and pride still remains the stumbling block that prevents me from loving the way others love.*

*My bones tell me that I miss you, my heart tells me that I love you and my head fights to understand the two. I continually try to make sense of my not so sensible actions and I am not entirely sure if I am willing to fight to change it. I seem to turn away from the type of sacrifice that is required in a relationship. Believing that I can escape from it or somehow be exempt from having to make it. I have tip-toed around it for some time now. Making minor changes to my routine when wholesale changes is what's required. I have found that it is easy to risk a little, when only little failures are possible. But it is very difficult to risk everything when failure could mean losing everything. Everything or nothing may sound like a cliché, but everything or nothing is the choice that I must face. I am scared. Scared that I will make a choice that I am not able to stay true to. Afraid to risk failure when failure is what is so clearly apparent in my mind.*

*I am coming to the realization that love trumps intimacy, that the ecstasy of sex will never be able to sustain the bound of a relation-ship. It is my resistance to accepting this reality that causes my actions to contradict my words. It's this defensive posture that is causing me to lose the fight. Constantly protecting myself and not being willing to swing forward to hit the thing that's been hitting me. My fear has frozen me and causes me to be knocked around the ring and occasionally onto the canvas. I have been unable to pro-tect all of my sensitive areas in my attempts to avoid getting hurt.*

*I do not have the words to explain the feeling of losing you. In part, my heart informs me that I've been here before. Yet another feeling I have is somewhat new. I'm facing the V in the road of this relationship and I don't have the luxury of time to make a proper decision. In facing my future, I foresee only two choices: I must give you everything you need and put me second or I must walk away from you and let go of everything I know you to be. In either case, a sacrifice is what's required and it's this sacrifice that I am failing to make.*

# NEVER SETTLE

~

*Never accept what your head advises you to accept. Want what you want and don't settle for anything other than that. Don't compromise what you believe will make you happy. Believe that the right person will come along. Believe that your wait will not be in vain. Trust your instincts and your judgment when evaluating your next love. Never settle.*

*You may never meet the person that best fit your personality. You may never have the dream relationship that you know that others have. Life may not taste as sweet as you hoped it would taste. Sometimes that's just the way things are. Don't be fooled into loving the one you're with and giving up on the one you want. It sounds nice in a song, but it is not a theory to live by. Fighting for what you want, waiting on what you believe in and believing what is to come, it's not just a motto, it's a battle cry. Just because you've never gotten it, doesn't mean you won't receive it. Life is not just about getting what you want; it's about fighting for happiness. Fighting for fairness in life. Hoping that your payday will come, given all of the hard work you have put in. Life is more about the walk and less about the arrival. Never settle.*

*Your parents may have shown you how relationships are to be handled. They may be the example that you strive to experience. It's what they have always known and they may not be able to recognize the dilemma that you find yourself in. They encourage you to wait, expect something great to come along and pray about it. Their words are valued but your life won't stand still. Your life is moving and waiting isn't working, wanting hasn't worked, and wishing is something that you have long given up on. You press for your significant other to walk into your life. So no stone is left unturned and every tea-leaf is evaluated. Each person you encounter is quickly measured to determine if your days of settling are over. Failures after failure your hopes are shattered. Each failure makes you wonder if your standards are too high. Maybe a little compromise is what's needed. Maybe some versatility is necessary. Your today begins to press upon your tomorrows. You consider all those that you have passed on, and begin to wonder if your decisions to pass on them were wise. Your second guesses are now your first guesses because your first guesses have left you with no one. No possibilities, no maybes and no one in the pipeline.*

*So somehow, someday, you do settle. You accept what is not for you. You give in to what you have pushed away from time and again. And in doing so, you get a little time, a little affection and some much needed appreciation. And if that's all you would have received before the relationship ends, then it may have been a good couple of weeks. But unfortunately, that's not all. In the weeks to follow you may get a little drama, a little STD and a little money gone down the drain. You may want to push to get your life going; you may want to press for the right person to arrive in your life. But what you should not do is settle.*

# CHAPTER VI

*Love is capable of healing the bruises of failure*

### Patience
*True love can never be rushed.*

### Show up soon
*Waiting is easiest when what you're expecting is on its way.*

### It's getting easier
*Never get comfortable with failure.*

### Beautiful
*In all things of nature, there is something of the marvelous.  Aristotle*

### Love is forever
*Once created; love can never be destroyed, only set aside.*

### Acknowledge me
*One man's trash is another man's treasure.*

### A love note
*Thoughts count when actions are not able to be seen.*

### Paycheck
*If the pay is worth it, then waiting should be expected.*

### Today is special
*tanding too close blinds you to that which is right in front of you.*

### Treat her right
*True love does not require love in return.*

### A new beginning
*Change starts from within and success comes from change.*

# PATIENCE

*I will give you patience even if it means your love. I have rushed into things far too many times, wanting only your body long before I even knew your last name. Before the paint had dried on our first conversation. Before ever telling you that you're beautiful. I had sought my own expectations instead of considering what you may one day choose to give freely. I had closed my mind to your tomorrows and only wanted to see your today.*

*I will give you patience so that you may find my soul, that elusive essence that tends to hide in the shadows of my life. My conscious. My upbringing. My character. The things that have taken a back seat to my morals. The things that can slow my run and force me to see what is within me. Those are the things that I have ignored in times past. Their absence has caused me to want only the physical you. Weighing all things against my ability to obtain that outside you. I have lacked the courage to enjoy that "old woman" in you, that inner you that will not change with the passage of time. You have asked for patience and I have said no to our future. No to giving you respect. No to being your partner. No to taking that journey with you that would last much longer than the pleasure of being with you.*

*I will give you patience even if my sacrifice will not yield me a reward. An outcome that I would have sought relentlessly in the past. I will give of myself in abundance and without expectation. My conversations with you will never cease. My excitement in your calls will never diminish. I will give of myself without reservation and expect only that you will receive it. Returning an occasional smile when it's appropriate, a laugh when it's deserved and a thank you when your heart tells you to say as much. I seek nothing more than the knowledge of knowing that I have treated you as well as another man would treat my own daughter. Seeking no more than what I expect my daughter to be given.*

*I will give you patience and will touch your heart gently when I handle it. Protect it from the constant strains of life and listen to the fast beats that I will cause when I give of my true self. Patience, I will give you patience. Your love is not a requirement. Your body will not be my goal. The times we will share together will be all that I will need to feed my lust. For I choose today, to only go where your mind lives. To that place that is not impressed with looks, words or style. To that place where smiles are created, laughter is encouraged and hands are touched softly. All that I will need to remain patient are all the things that we will share together. I have pushed too hard, for far too long. Pushing past our first laugh and rushing through our first hug. Focusing on the parts of you that are sure to change and not seeking out that you that will never change. Today I pledge to you, patience. The ability to focus on you, on us and on that journey that will determine if "we" should ever even be. My reward will be to give you true friendship. My quest will be to show you the man that I am and my failure can only be that I was not able to give you the patience you needed to relax in my presence. To allow you to let your guard down long enough so I could see your inner smile. If I should fail, then I will fail myself. Losing my only chance to deposit the true me in you. So you can expect patience from me, even if it means I will never receive your love.*

# SHOW UP SOON

~

I'm expecting her to show up soon. I've been waiting on her for some time now, pushing away the wannabes and holding back the could-bees. I've been trying to fight the good fight, trying to stay grounded in the airport of life while others takeoff and land all around me. My wait is trying me. Trying my faith, trying my patience and trying my ability to be true. Totally true. True to my expectations of that which I am waiting for.

But, I'm still expecting her to show up soon. Not in a fancy car, wearing a nice outfit or even with a job that shows her independence. I wait simply for her to arrive on the scene. Nothing more and nothing less. To show herself. To make herself known to the hopes that are hidden within me. I expect her to be confused. She may not be aware that she is the coming attraction. She may not be aware that her normal is my excitement. Her today is my Christmas time. So it's clear, she will not accept me immediately. She will see her flaws and I will see her exceptions. Her blemishes which have shaped her character. The hidden beauty that pours out of her on those ordinary days to reveal the never-changing her, the ageless her. The her that she yearns to be.

I'm still expecting her to show up soon though. Feeling her way through life like a blind man crossing a busy street. Listening for the sounds and processing the information that his eyes cannot see. Wondering if it's safe, wishing only to have a trusting hand, but not asking to be carried. She arrives with her insecurities still intact. She arrives with her failures still fresh in her mind and her mistakes still visible to the trained eye. Is it me? Am I the one? She will wonder if the impossible has really arrived in her life. She will wonder and be very afraid. Her expectations have always been nothing more than a fantasy. Her body will meet me and ask for patience. Her mind will meet me and ask me for everything. She will be torn between her physical and her emotions and she won't like her choices. I secretly wish I could tell her that it will be the only pain that I will ever cause her.

*But, I'm still expecting her to show up soon. I have made plans for our tomorrows, for our possibilities, for our celebrations. She only needs to bring willingness to love, the chance to be hurt and the courage to risk failing again. Giving just a little will not be an option. She will have to want be in love more than her fear of being hurt by love. She'll have to stand in a crowded room with her arms stretched wide and say "I'll love again." Not someone old, but someone new. A stranger, someone not currently known to her that will require her to love once again. She will have to expose herself and she will have to do it before she's ready. Her visions of this day will not be what she had expected. She had expected him to float down on a cloud of roses, but he'll be walking in shoes that have been worn a day too long. His armor will not be visible to the naked eye. His strength will not be apparent in the things that he will be carrying. She will seek her future and her wait will be in vain. It will not be until she closes her eyes and opens her heart for his true power to reveal itself. She will then let her guard down and accept what she is to receive. He will arrive on the scene with his heart open and she will find her way in, so I'm expecting her to show up soon.*

# IT'S GETTING EASIER

*Waking up alone, sitting in my room alone, living in my home alone. I don't like it and I hope I never get used to it. I want it to end, cease, be over and never be this way again. Because being this way seems to be destroying a part of me. How can I get used to being my own supporter, my own confidant, a partner to myself? It's difficult trying to be objective when the voice of reason is your voice. I hear only echoes. The sounds that sound like the sounds that I make. I am the man in the mirror and this face is not the face I want to see, but it's getting easier.*

*I know what it is to love, but I am losing my ability to love. I am tightening my grip on my willingness to let go. I am becoming afraid of the possible. My shortened conversations about nothing is what is talked about, while my deeper conversations about life is what is expected from me. All efforts to open my heart up and let my soul pour out has been met with resistance. My frustration is boiling over and my patience is running short. It's been too long. I have been punished enough but enough never stops. I work more now. I focus more now. What one man has too much of, I don't have enough of, but it's getting easier. My expectations go no further than the next twenty-four hours. My hopes are whispered in silence. My envy of others is a daily struggle that I try to hide. I resent others for the things that I do not have. Wanting to get lucky or just a little bit lucky, just to get a bit of what's missing in my life. Maybe get a little of something to use as fuel so that I can get to the location where my destiny awaits. But even so, it's getting easier.*

*The curve in the road, the bend in the line. That junction in life that kick-starts your hopes. The paddles that would cause your flat line to wiggle again. It's getting easier to predict. To simply accept today as my tomorrow and live the same way. The same as before. Doing nothing on most days, very little on special days and making no plans for my future days. It is what I cannot change, my life, my situation, my today. There are chains around my neck that tie me to the way things are and it's getting easier that way. It gives me something to point to, somewhere to run from. A cause that fits this effect and it's getting easier.*

*I have tried to write my way out. Begging for help through poetry and trying to lead a horse to water that's not ready to drink. My life raft is sinking and instead of letting go of it I'm holding on to it for dear life, but it's getting easier to let go.*

◖ *Sylvester Hubbard III*

# BEAUTIFUL

~

*How else can I describe her? I could look within her soul and call her loving. I could talk to her friends and call her faithful. I could even watch her through the eyes of multiple strangers and call her versatile. But I choose to describe her as beautiful. The way her dimples merge together to make the perfect face. The way her pearly whites slightly touch when she brightens the room with her smile. I even envision the way her eyebrows curl inward, but never to make a frowning face. I could tell you she looks nice or that she has a pleasant personality. I could even say that she has a down-to-earth type attitude. But that wouldn't describe her as well as the word, beautiful.*

*I have tried to turn away on occasion hoping not to be overtaken by her normal. Knowing that any effort from her to give any more, would cause me to overdose. To overload my senses and cause me to want things that she has not yet offered. I am careful not to want too much, too soon. Her playful demeanor gives you a false sense of togetherness. It leads you to believe, that you are receiving something special. Something different from that which others have received. Her normal is misleading. It is more then you are used to, but not something to be used to measure your closeness with her. So you're left imagining what it would be like to receive her special, her above normal responses and having only your imagination as a guide, it fascinates you. The thoughts of her not-so-normal attention excite you and for lack of the ability to describe it, you call it beautiful.*

*You imagine her laugh, which is always on time and is always yearned for. It lights the darkest of rooms and it can even be seen in silence. I know this to be true because I have heard it ring from miles away, when she reads funny text messages. Her laugh is like music, it soothes the savage beast that is within. She alone is her own symphony. Her laugh, her voice and her cheering can be compared to the playing of pianos, flutes and trumpets in an orchestra. They allow her to make noises like Beethoven when she laughs and they are nothing short of beautiful.*

*Even her style, her fashion sense and the way she envisions the unseen things in you are remarkable. She coordinates colors like that of Picasso. She adorns herself with fabrics envied by Versace and her ability to compliment your personality can only be compared to the writing of Maya Angelou. It's simply beautiful. Her inner style far outweighs her intelligence, her versatility and her ability to reason. She is confident and courageous. She is able to see herself in the very way she portrays herself. She knows that she is far from perfect, yet she is still able to live life without second guessing herself. She's metamorphic, able to adjust without changing who she is and able to protect herself and still reach out to you. She is the dream that men hate to wake up from. She is that pot of gold that sits at the end of every rainbow. She is truly beautiful. If I am missing a characteristic to describe her or if I have not completely explained what she looks like then forgive me. If there is a hole in her attitude that I have failed to fill, then I will fill it with beautiful. If there is a situation pertaining to her that's not quite understood, I will lace it with beautiful. I will never hesitate to fill in the pieces of the puzzle or complete the writing on the wall. I will finish every sentence that has already been started about her with beautiful. It describes not just what you see in her, it is what you cannot see in her. It is simply the word you should use in describing that special person in your life. The word to be used when you don't understand something in the relationship. The word that should be used when imagining your future together. Beautiful. Don't just use it as an adjective to describe what you can or cannot see. It should be better thought of as an attitude. An attitude that reflects how you should interact with her, how you should deal with her or how you should think of her. So the next time understanding fails in the relationship or compromise doesn't seem work things out, try beautiful. It will straighten your eyebrows, soften your touch and lower your tone. It's the attitude that reminds you that what you see in her, what you know about her and who she is, is simply beautiful.*

# LOVE IS FOREVER

~

*Moving on doesn't diminish it and letting go doesn't destroy it. It comes back like cancer and sticks around like an old cousin wanting some money. Love is persistent. It leaves for short periods of time, then comes back with a vengeance. Throwing monkey wrenches in your plans for today and your thoughts for tomorrow. Money can only distract you from it for so long. Taking vacations or weekend getaways don't do much to help ease the pain of love. They serve only to get your mind away from it, but in the end you only find yourself away from home thinking about the reasons you not at home.*

*You search for a replacement love, believing that will help destroy your past love. Your search is awkward because you find yourself wanting to jump quick and deep into a new love to ease the pain of your past love. Wanting only to immerse yourself in something to help brace your emotions, knowing full well of the firestorm that your actions are sure to cause. It is very difficult knowing you have the power of a tsunami bottled up inside you. Wanting to unleash this love on someone that has the basic ingredients to love you back. Someone that will jump into the water to save you, while all along risking their own emotions and knowing full well that they cannot swim. Electing to get into the water anyway, believing that together two poor swimmers can dogpaddle their way to safety. You meet the stranger and want or even expect them to jump in because you need to be rescued just that badly. Having rejected any sort of charity in the past, you look for it now. You'll take it willingly without the thought of whether or not you deserve it.*

*You have looked at this forever love and contemplated ways you can get over it, past it or maybe even through it. Nothing has worked to weaken it. This love is right there in your face and it pisses you off because the one whose love you cannot let go of, is blinded by stupidity. You become angry at moments knowing that you are the only one going though this detox. The twelve step program is not working and you are yet to muster the courage to move on. You want to, but cannot even find a new love willing to take the journey with you. It is through this failure and your understanding of the pains of love that you have found a way out. A door that may be large enough to get you on the backside of love.*

*Indebtedness. That's the door. The debt being your life, your peace of mind and your ability to be. You search for someone that will risk loving you because you need to be loved. Someone able to see the tsunami in you and is able to swim. Someone that can take a few bumps and bruises up front and stay strong long enough to receive the prize that's sure to come. You need someone to be there for you and stay there long enough to see you through. You need someone that you will owe your future to. A debt that will take you a lifetime to repay. It's the only substance that can diminish that "forever love" that you are failing to let go of.*

# ACKNOWLEDGE ME

~

*You've forgotten about me. The lost soul in your life. The forever constant that has been consistent in your life for years now. You have overlooked my presence, you have bypassed my feelings and you have ignored my existence for far too long. I am here, so acknowledge me.*

*I have raised your kids, I have supported your ideals and I have loved your faults. I have been here waiting to be loved by you for some time now, patiently hoping to become the most important aspect in your life. My scream sounds like a soft hug or a gentle kiss. My patience is beyond measure. I have stood by you long enough, waiting and wanting to be the center of your life. Not just when you are down, depressed or having feelings of loneliness, but also during your successes. Those days you're smiling, laughing and traveling down the winding roads of life. I'm here during those times as well, so acknowledge me.*

*Allow me to be your day in and day out centerpiece. Your in good times and in bad times centerpiece. The one that your heart is built upon and your future is geared toward. Recognize me as your help mate. The one that's been here all along, helping you to do what you do, the way you've been doing it. Credit my unconditional love for keeping you grounded, my unwavering loyalty for giving you strength and my unquestioned devotion that has brought you peace. Recognize that I have fought for us and for our love to transcend time. I am reminded of those times when I fought the fight for the both of us, when I endured the pain for the both us and on those days I accepted the blame for the both of us. Realize that it is my loyalty that allows you to not worry when man after man begs me to be their woman. Realize that it is my commitment that remained constant when you were caught in a situation the caused me to lose trust in you. I did that. Not for you, not for me, but for us, so acknowledge me.*

*I'm not just a holiday trophy, an occasionally fling or a once-in-a-while lover. I am permanent, forever and I am here to stay. I am your woman, the one that you have taken for granted day in and day out. Year after year I have become less of person in your life.*

*I have not changed, you have just gotten use to me. Your memory has faded and you need to be reminded of the way things used to be. You seem to be no longer concerned about the queen in your life. I know that you love me; you've just forgotten to show me that you love me. You don't wake up any more trying to think of ways to make me laugh. You don't stare at me anymore when I walk around in a skimpy outfit or even when I wear something sexy to touch your thoughts. My curves don't seem to have the same effect on you that they once had. Pushing me away has become the norm and it hurts me. Your desire for me is not just a physical want, it's an emotional need. You're still my superman and I am still head-over-hills-in-love with you, both physically and emotionally. My love for you has gotten stronger over the years and your love for me seems to have leveled out. You can't stop loving me now. You can't stop needing me now. You are all I have and I have never prepared for a plan B. You must not forget that I am here, so acknowledge me.*

*You're no longer threatened when other men look at me in an enticing way. You trust my loyalty without question. Your comfort has become my curse. I've been taken for granted and you don't see it. Nothing I have said or done has made you understand that you are hurting me. So I'm informing you of my misery today. I am stating my objections to the person that you have become and I am asking you to wake up from your long sleep and once again recognize me as the love of your life. Love me once again with the love of our first kiss and the romance of our first date. Give me back the man that spent his every waking moment doing whatever he could to show me that I was the one. Do this for me now because your actions, your words and this feeling I have are beginning to convince me that you've forgotten about me. But on the contrary, I am here, so acknowledge me.*

# A LOVE NOTE

~

*I want to tell you, I love you. It has been pressing on my mind for some time now. Since that time long ago when I decided I would do things right, try things in the right way and be the right man. Meeting you has awakened me from a long sleep. My eyes are wide open and I find myself startled. I am reminded of the last time this occurred in me. It happened the day of my birth. Like today, I awoke from a long sleep and found myself amazed at how things had changed. Things that were so very different just a few moments prior. Both events happened without my knowledge and neither of these events am I able to explain.*

*I want to tell you, I love you. That my wait for you was not without its ups and downs. On several occasions, I have tried settling for someone other than you. My settling did fail and although I am here now, those failures almost caused me to miss your arrival. So it pleases me to recognize that in revealing yourself to me you have opened my eyes to those things that my words have failed to describe. You are everything; you are all that I need to be able to love all that I can. I offer you all of me. I lay my heart at your feet and wait anxiously for you to pick it up. To take it into your arms and hold it tight. Your ability to hold on to it is of no concern to me. I ask only that you touch it just a little. Hold it just a little. Allow yourself to search within it and know that my words are true. Wrap your arms around my heart just long enough so that you can hear its beats. Beats that will echo in the corridors of your dreams. Find comfort in knowing that a guarantee is not what I require. A chance is all that I ask for. If only for a moment in your arms, my wait will not have been in vain.*

*I want to tell you, I love you. That meeting you has quieted my desires for all others. It has destroyed the temptations that have controlled me in the past. I have found the cure to all of my weaknesses and I have found that cure in you. You have cured me without giving me any medicines, without strange herbs and without touching me. Without you giving me anything, your presence has given me everything. For this, allow me to hold you tightly. To squeeze you close to that which beats within me. My heart is alive again and the sound that it is now making is music to my ears.*

*I want to tell you, I love you. That even the words I write fall short of the message I am trying to give. I am trying to say "uncle" to the person that has an advantage over me. "I give up" to the person that has chased me to the point that I am exhausted and "you win" to the one that has scored the game winning shot. That even these initial moments are more than enough to change what I have once thought to be unchangeable. It makes my heart want to scream in your ears and have it echo throughout your substance. These words are meant to touch your heart in places that my hands could never reach. So I want to tell you, I love you because my hands will fail to reach the part of you that has made my dreams a reality.*

# PAYCHECK

~

It happened today. About twenty minutes before twelve I decided to give her what she has been asking for. To release to her that thing that she has been yearning to receive for some time now and allow her full access to the whole enchilada. To give her everything that was held back from her in the past and open the door once and for all, so that her constant knocking will be silenced. It was now all hers to sleep with, hers to travel with, hers to talk with and hers to grow old with.

Today, I decided to love her back. Not just in words, hopes or maybes, but in deeds. Deeds that can be seen with the eye, touched by the hand and felt in the heart. Today, I opened up the storehouse and allowed her to eat to her heart's content. She had told me time and again that she was hungry. She had told me time and again of her desires and had insisted that she be let in and allowed to eat. She had pressed upon me in moments of depression to allow her to help me. She had pressed upon me in times of loneliness to allow her to be present. She had told me many times that my secrets would be safe with her. That my insecurities would be kept close and that she will protect them with her dying breath. She has waited for quite a while now and many times before today her wait was in vain. She had once seen the smorgasbord that's locked within me, but never had she been allowed to enjoy the food. No more. Her fight to receive has been hard fought, bloody and has left her with a lifetime of painful memories, but no more. Today is her victory party. Today she will do her victory dance and laugh at the top of her lungs. All that she deserves and all that she has waited for will be at her finger tips. Goosebumps will pop-up on her arms and the hair on the back of her neck will stand. The shivers she feels will not be due to a cool breeze or a sudden bang of a pistol, it will be from her excitement. She's giddy now, like a school girl being chased by the little school boy carrying a frog.

"This is what life is supposed to be like," she says within herself. This is how she is to be loved. So she pinches herself to be sure that she is not dreaming and she smiles as she listens to the little voice within saying, "This is my man." A sense of peace will come over her when she realizes that her vacation driver has been determined. Her retirement partner has been established and she can now sleep peacefully when she hears a bump in the night. To her delight, she has met her last lover and it happened just before noon today. She will waste little time thinking about why today was so special. Her request for a feast was no greater today than it had been on any other occasion. She was not dressed to the tee, it was not sunny outside and there were no "End of the world" predictions that she knew of. Nothing, absolutely nothing had changed that she could point to. But unbeknownst to her, at twenty till noon today, I had changed. And in doing so she was now able to receive the pay that she had been working for year after year. So at about twenty minutes before noon today on a cool Friday morning, she was delivered her pay check. It was addressed to her, it was signed by me and the dollar amount written on the check read, "I'm yours!"

*The special treatment that you expect is not something that you can expect daily. I can't treat you special every day. Making you smile is not always the number one thing on my to-do list. Your past relationships are not my past relationships. I can only be me. A simple man with simple ideals. The by-product of my own successes and my own failures. Trying daily to carry my own cross and unable to bear your cross as well. Your request to be made to feel special on a daily basis is too much for me. It serves only as a reminder of your past and warns me to be cautious. A warning sign of things to come and things that may never come. You not only tell me with you actions, you tell me through your words. Words like, "I love hard." In them, you are advising me of your quest to be sure in your next relationship. Planning your future on nothing short of a guarantee. Seeking a microwave man that is ready to go. A man that will move at your speed, fast on emotions and slow on intimacy. A man that's emotionally supernatural. An aberration of nature. You have looked within your past and found a set of qualities that would fit your current state of mind. A wish list that will be used as a measuring stick for all men to come. A measuring stick that will measure his giving so that you may grade his commitment.*

*The special treatment that you expect is not something that you could be given daily. The friends you have, have misled you. They have lead you into believing that their smiles and their laughter are new each and every day. They are not. Many of their smiles are leftover thoughts that still touch their hearts when spoken upon. It's the afterglow of a deed, event or set of words that continue to sit upon their lips. You have mistakenly believed that these smiles of today, are from today. You want to believe it, because you want to believe in fairly tales. Ideal relationships that you have only seen from the outside. Never knowing the work and sacrifice that was built over time to create them. Your mind has been involved in a hoax. An impractical set of events played upon you by your own ego. Misconceptions reinforced by your family and your close friends. It was not vicious. It was just misinformed. They told you only of the victories that they had won. All of their failures, misunderstandings, bitterness and anger was pushed under the rug and never told to you. Fight your urge and resist your instincts, of believing a perfect relationship is possible. A perfect relationship is not possible, it is only a failed relationship that has weathered the test of time. A relationship that chose to cultivate forgiveness and did not take the easy way out. This is the reality that you have failed to comprehend. The reality that all good relationships have been bad relationships at one time or another.*

*The special treatment that you expect is not something that you can expect daily. It cannot be found in books and magazines and it cannot be duplicated by cloning the events that have occurred in the relationships of others. The daily special that you seek is not daily at all. It can sometimes be seen on a given day or even on a series of days, but this is not the daily special that you seek or even should seek. That special that you see in the relationships that you respect runs much deeper. It's a special that exists in knowing that through thick and thin you are loved. That in trials and trivializations your man will never contemplate leaving. That giving up is never the first option; it's the very last option. The special that you fail to realize knows that you are loved more than his desires for others and other things. This daily special that you are failing to see is your inability to comprehend his existence in your life today and his desire to remain there in your tomorrows. I will never be able to treat you special every day but I will be in your life hoping that every day I am here, our special would have endured yet another day.*

# TREAT HER RIGHT

~

*Treat her like she wants to be treated. Give to her the time and attention that she requires. Allow her the opportunity to see the man in you before ever asking for some intimacy. Invest the time and resources in her to help her shake off her past failed relationships. Convince her with your actions, that you are going to give her 100 percent and that you will do so according to her rules and on her time table. Do these things because she is deserving of it and not because she may possibly become your woman. She may just need some unfairness in her life. She may be long overdue for some confidence building. She may have been shorted in times past, and this time she wants what she feels she is owed. Some love, some attention and some patience. Her past relationships have failed and she needs help trusting again, reasons to give again and ways to accept a man's love once again. Her gentleness is what she is protecting. She knows that things are not going to be fair or balanced in the beginning. She knows that your time and finances will be put to the test. She is not delusional in what she believes you expect from her. She wants it just as much as you do. You struggle to get it and she fights to preserve it. You both want the same things; only she wants to give it in abundance. She wants to be sure that you will accept it more than once, more than a little while and more than a couple of years. Her patience can be measured in how long she is able to resist her own desires.*

*She asks only that you treat her in the way she needs to be treated. To laugh with her on a regular basis. To spend time with her in those moments when intimacy is not what's being sought after. Show her the old fashioned way your grandfather took pride in doing things right, and in the right way. The dating period is not a game. It's the appetizer before the big meal, the pep-talk before the big game or the studying prior to taking an exam. Your attention is needed as a confirmation to what your words have proclaimed you to be. She may ask to be treated this way, but you must realize for yourself, that she needs to be treated that way. Show her your strength by showing her your willingness to give without restrictions, your willingness to communicate without coercion and your ability to accept her without her having to change. Do these things and you will never have to worry about her love, her kindness or her commitment. You would have given her what she needs and treated her in a way she has needed to be treated. She will not just appreciate it, she will fall in love with it. She will in return, be open to spending the rest of her life trying to treat you in the very way you have wanted to be treated. So treat her right.*

# A NEW BEGINNING

~

*It's never easy at the beginning. Starting over from scratch, trying to become someone new, someone that you've always wanted to be. Wanting to develop a new attitude, a new flow and even new hang-out spots. You tend to fight it for years. Never wanting to be something that you're not. So you fight against change even when change is necessary for you to grow. You question your character and believe that if you do change, would that change make you a phony? Would you become someone that has changed to project an image that is based on the bruises that life has given you. So again and again you avoid making those changes that would make you happy. You push them aside and hope that the world around you changes instead.*

*You imagine what it would take to create yourself a new beginning. So looking within yourself you realize that you must contend with cutting the unnecessary pieces from your life. Like pruning a flower, you are never sure if you'll cut away some of the beauty while cutting away the dead spots. You have never had a green thumb, so your hesitation seems warranted. And even while looking into your past, you have seen the dead spots, you have also seen how they have been eating away at the good spots in your life. The dead spots seem to be so close to the good spots that your cutting will ultimately put your good spots in jeopardy. It is also not so obvious to you, if all of the bad spots should even go. They seem to be character builders, life's lessons and warning sighs. They're everywhere, and with so much dead and so little beauty, you worry if the flower will survive. Will it be able to live beyond this pruning process? Will there be enough left for you to grow again or should you just destroy the flower and plant new seeds altogether?*

*An emotional change will always come without warning signs. We accept it, dissect it and fight with it. It is our conscious. It breaks our sleep at night when we ignore it, it removes the words from our mouths when we try to explain it and it is what we all run from when poor decisions have been made. It is our gate-keeper that stands between good and evil. To not allow it to have its way would cause us to do evil to our brothers and unspeakable things to others. The lack of it makes us ruthless and cold, and to ignore if for a length of time would cause us to become numb and prevent us from enjoying the sensations of love. The lack of this consciousness is what produces misery and over time we begin to hate our lives and search for a ways to start over again.*

*The search for a new path is not as easy as others would lead you to believe. The paths are right there in front of you but you must change who you are to walk on them. You must twist and turn the person that you are so that your walk will not be the same walk you've walked in times past. The path looks the same, the curves seem no different and the bends have a familiar twist. So it is not the fear of the unknown that grips you and causes you to pause, it's the fear of encountering this unknown with a different purpose, with a different attitude and with a greater potential to fail. You have not faced devastation for years and you memory of it continues to conjure up thoughts of bitterness.*

*Yet, you search for a new beginning and your search has led you to this point. A point that requires you to let go of what you know so that you may grab hold of what's to come. A point that requires you to fall first and grab hold second. It's not something that comes naturally to any of us. To let go of all that you know, good and bad and risk grabbing something new. It's not an easy thing, but to begin anew, you must stand at this crossroads in life and convince yourself to turn away from the direction you're headed. You must face a never before seen road and walk down a path that has never before been traveled. And you must do it with the simple hope of receiving a small piece of joy. Just enough to encourage you to take your first step into what will be, your new beginning.*

CPSIA information can be obtained at www.ICGtesting.com
Printed in the USA
BVOW042224290412

288887BV00001B/5/P